Frozen Footprints

*Lessons in Freedom from a Survivor
of the Siberian Slave-Labor Camps*

Frozen Footprints
*Lessons in Freedom from a Survivor
of the Siberian Slave-Labor Camps*

by Alicia Gilewicz

Printed in the United States of America
First Edition, July 1998

ISBN 0-9632667-8-0

Published by INTI Publishing
Tampa, FL

Cover design by Laurie Winters
Layout by Bayou Graphics

Dedication

This book is dedicated in loving memory to my father, Joseph; to my loving and supportive husband, Hank; to our two wonderful sons, Michael and Mark; and to my mother, Janina, who taught me to always reach for the stars.

Acknowledgments

I'd like to give glory and honor to my Father in heaven and to Jesus Christ, my Lord and Savior. I'd like to thank my son Mark, who had the vision for this wonderful book and who worked countless hours to see that vision through to the end.

I'd also like to thank my dear friend Burke Hedges and the entire staff at INTI Publishing, especially Steve Price and Katherine Glover.

Most of all I'd like to thank all of the freedom fighters throughout the world who paid the ultimate price of giving their lives so that we may continue to be free.

Foreword

At times I find it hard to believe that the warm, loving person I call my mother was actually a prisoner in a Siberian slave-labor camp. Each time I re-read the horrors my mother endured in Russia, I am amazed at this seven-year-old girl's determination to survive, and I feel privileged to be her son.

I've been doubly blessed in life, first for having the good fortune to have Hank and Alicia Gilewicz as my parents; and second to have been the child of Amway Diamonds. The business enabled my parents to achieve financial freedom, which in turn afforded them the opportunity to travel around the world and make a difference in so many lives. I'm honored to share in their mission and to pass on the torch of freedom for as long as I live.

I hope that after reading this book, you will not just put it aside and forget the message. I hope that you, too, join my family and me to fight oppression and spread the message of freedom to every corner of the world.

The Apostle Paul says, "I have fought the good fight, I have finished the race, I have kept the faith..." Over the years I have witnessed my mother living Paul's inspiring words in her endless crusade for freedom. I pledge to continue "fighting the good fight" alongside my parents for many years to come. May that be your goal in life, as well.

— Mark Gilewicz

Contents

Introduction
Never Take Freedom for Granted!

> *Give me your tired,*
> *your poor,*
> *your huddled masses,*
> *yearning to be free.*
>
> — from the poem on the
> base of the Statue of Liberty

The story I'm about to tell you isn't a pretty one. I know because it happened to me.

It's a story about an innocent seven-year-old girl and her devoted parents, trapped in the frozen killing fields of Eastern Europe during World War II.

It's a story about what happens when the darkest demons of human nature — hate, anger, power, and intolerance — are encouraged and nurtured, instead of restrained.

It's a story of mass starvation ... mass murder ... mass graves ... and mass misery.

Most of all, it's a story about what can happen when your freedom is stolen from you.

Freedom Is Never Free
You could say I've lived a real-life fairy tale. Like the innocent

children in the classic fairy tale *Hansel and Gretel*, the early chapters of my life-story were filled with terror and the constant threat of death. Fortunately, fairy tales have happy endings. And so does my real-life fairy tale.

Today I live in a beautiful home on a lovely lake in the freest country in the world. I've been blessed with a loving husband, Hank, and two wonderful children, Michael and Mark. My husband and I have the financial freedom to come and go as we please.

But as you will discover from reading this book, my freedom wasn't handed to me on a silver platter. My family and I had to pay a very dear price for our freedom. Was our freedom worth the price we paid? Absolutely! Freedom is everything to me, and I'll never, ever take it for granted!

What You Will Learn from Reading This Book

In the first section of this book, I'll tell you about eight horrible years in my childhood, from ages seven to 15, when survival was a daily struggle, first as prisoners in a Siberian prison camp and later as refugees in Russia, Iran, and Africa. During this brief but brutal period in history, one-third of the "educated elite" in Poland lost their lives. All told, six million Polish citizens lost their lives during World War II.

My family and I were among those fortunate few who managed to survive. In one sense this book is a eulogy to the millions of innocent people who were smashed into submission or murdered by the blunt hammer of communism. The story of my lost innocence is worth telling, if for no other reason than to remind people that we must honor our hard-won freedoms and safeguard them so that a child will never again experience the unspeakable horrors I lived through more than 50 years ago.

Frozen Footprints is a living testimony to the virtue of freedom and to the fact that if we remain vigilant and take a stand FOR individual freedoms and AGAINST oppressive governments everywhere, good can, indeed, triumph over evil.

Perhaps by telling you about the horrors I experienced as a child at the hands of the communists, I can transfer my passion for freedom to you. Perhaps my story will encourage more people to *stop taking their freedoms for granted!*

Voluntary Slaves in America

Eventually, of course, my family found freedom from the Siberian salve-labor camps and the tyranny of communism. Our search for freedom ultimately led us to "the Land of the Free" — America — where I followed the conventional formula for success. I went to college, studied hard, and graduated with a bachelor of science degree. In my early 20s I married Hank Gilewicz, a bright, ambitious engineer.

Within a few short years Hank and I were living the American Dream — or so I thought. We had two wonderful sons and a beautiful house in the suburbs. We belonged to one of the most exclusive country clubs in town. Then, one day, I realized — perhaps *admitted* is a better word — that we weren't really free after all. We had traded our freedom to a corporation for a "secure job." We'd become voluntary slaves to IBM and Hank's demanding boss!

"Hank," I used to say, "my parents and I used to dream about coming to America and living free. Our dream of living in this great country came true, *but we still aren't free!*

"We don't really control our lives, Hank," I continued. "The truth is your boss and IBM control our lives. We don't make the important financial decisions in our life — *they do!* We don't decide how much income we earn — *they do!* We don't decide where we are going to live — *they do!* Hank, there's got to be a way to take control of our destiny instead of letting someone else control it."

Dont' get me wrong — I wasn't knocking jobs. Everybody's got to work to earn a living for themselves and their families, and there are lots of great, challenging jobs that pay a good wage. But let's face it, when you have a job, no matter how great it is, you don't call the shots. Someone else does.

Hank and I felt that the key to controlling our lives was to go into business for ourselves. But there were always big drawbacks to every business we looked at. Usually the start-up cost or the risk was too high. So we kept looking and hoping for the right opportunity.

In 1972 we discovered the vehicle that would deliver us to freedom. We were introduced to the Amway business. It took us five years to become Diamond Directs and for Hank to "escape" from his job, and by 1977, we were finally the captains of our own ship. We were finally free.

It's amazing that, after all I'd been through, in a sense I had still taken freedom for granted for the first 20 years in this country! No more! The good news is that for the last 25 years, Hank and I have worked and lived as free citizens in this great, free country of ours, and I can tell you, we'll never live any other way again!

Section Two: 10 Lessons in Freedom

The best news is that people don't have to remain voluntary slaves in America if they don't want to. Hank and I aren't exceptional people. Tens of thousands of people have taken control of their lives and are enjoying the same freedoms we enjoy! All it takes is a willingness to learn the system ... work the business ... and to keep going until you accomplish your dream.

That's what the second section of this book is all about. It contains the 10 fundamental life lessons that people must learn and practice in order to take full advantage of the enormous benefits of free enterprise through the Amway opportunity.

I first learned these lessons as a child while struggling to survive in a frozen wasteland called Siberia. I've applied these 10 lessons countless times over the years, and they've never failed me. I can say beyond a shadow of a doubt that if you apply these lessons to your personal and professional life, you will experience freedom in ways you could never imagine.

Like I said earlier, freedom isn't free. You have to exercise your freedoms by voting. You have to put your freedoms into practice by making your own decisions ... running your own life ... operating your own business ... and standing up and speaking out when someone or something threatens your freedom.

Melting the Frozen Footprints in Your Life

As for me, I've seen frozen footprints in the snow — bloody footprints that ended at a rusted barbed wire fence surrounding a lonely labor camp in Siberia. On the other side of the fence were full trees and wide rivers and proud mountains. But no footprints. They all ended at the angry fence.

Fortunately, the *external fences* of communism and fascism

are being torn down all over the world. Unfortunately, the *internal fences* that people voluntarily build around themselves are still holding many of us back.

Fences of fear.

Fences of hopelessness.

Fences of untapped potential.

Fences of self-doubt.

Fences of ignorance.

I pray that my struggle for freedom will inspire you to tear down the self-limiting fences that are holding you back from enjoying *total freedom* — spiritual freedom ... physical freedom ... and financial freedom.

I pray that this book will light a fire within you that will warm your heart and thaw your courage, and, in so doing, will melt the frozen footprints in your life.

Section 1
Lost Innocence

1

"You're Under Arrest!"

My real-life nightmare began on a cold February morning in 1940 in our home just outside Dubno, a charming, historic city in eastern Poland less than 50 miles from the Russian border.

I thought I heard loud pounding noises at our front door.

BOOM! BOOM! BOOM!

Was I awake or was I dreaming?

BOOM! BOOM! BOOM!

"Mommy, is that you? What's that noise? Am I awake? Or is this a bad dream?"

BOOM! BOOM! BOOM!

"It's all right, Alicia. Everything will be fine," my mother said softly as she hugged me close, rocking me gently back and forth, trying her best to reassure both of us.

"Your father is taking care of everything," she said. "There's nothing to worry about." But her voice was strained with fear.

BOOM! BOOM! BOOM!

Cold, hard voices pierced the door like bullets.

"Pod scienku, ruki v vier! Sobierajsia s vieszczami!"

"Hands up. Pack your things!"

I soon realized the banging came from Russian soldiers pounding their rifle butts against the front door. The loud voices were inside now, as cold and hard as iron.

Suddenly, I was awake — wide awake.

But this wasn't the end of a child's nighttime dream.

This was the beginning of long, long nightmare!

"Pack your things. You're under arrest!"

My mother and father had dreaded this day, but deep inside they knew it was inevitable.

By the time we heard the pounding of rifle butts against our front door, Poland was caught in the jaws of two rabid, power-hungry dogs named Adolph Hitler and Joseph Stalin. During the summer of 1939, these two ruthless dictators had worked out a secret pact to partition Poland between them.

Germans and Russians Strike

On September 1, 1939, Germany invaded Poland from the west in what came to be known as a *blitzkrieg* — a lightning war. The Polish army was no match for the German war machine, and the Nazis controlled west and central Poland within days.

Then, without warning, Russia attacked eastern Poland only 19 days after the German invasion from the west. The Red army rolled its tanks and trucks across the Polish-Soviet frontier with little resistance. By nightfall Dubno and all the surrounding villages were overrun with Soviet soldiers. Following a brief military administration, the dreaded Soviet Secret Police (better known today as the KGB) took control of the country.

Arrested for "Crimes Against the People"

The Communists' first order of business was to purge the population of all "undesirables" for "committing crimes against the people." Within weeks, hundreds of thousands of innocent, law-abiding Polish citizens were arrested. Almost overnight all businesses, industries, and personal properties were nationalized. Every political official was arrested, and more than 15,000 officers in the Polish military were taken to the Katyn Forest and massacred.

Next the Communists arrested doctors, lawyers, and teachers. Property owners were labeled as capitalists. They were arrested and their property was seized by the communist government. Educated citizens were labeled as elitists. They were arrested and their books and papers were burned. In many cases, school children who had shown any loyalty to Poland were seized by the KGB. Some were snatched from their families as they walked down the streets.

As the arrests escalated, the nation's social structure was thrown into total chaos. Electricity was shut off. Water pipes burst. Sewers backed up. Epidemics raged. Conditions were so bad that thousands of political prisoners died from starvation or neglect before they were brought to "trial."

Living in Constant Fear

Everyone in Poland had heard the whispered stories about mass executions and Soviet death camps. In 1940, if you lived in Poland, the threat of imprisonment and death was all around you. To live in Poland in 1940 was to live in fear. Men looked over their shoulders at work. Women shopped quickly, with their heads down. Everybody hurried to get home before dark.

This was the backdrop to my story. This was communism in action.

Then in February, my family's worst fears became reality. The communists ordered mass deportations of the "undesirables," which meant any Polish citizen in a position of influence. The communists' first rule of order was to eliminate what they called *the intelligentsiya,* that is, the educated or enlightened class.

Because my parents were considered upper middle class, it was just a matter of time before the communists came for us. My father, Joseph, worked for the forestry service, and my mother, Janina, was trained as a horticulturist. The stated goal of the communists was to create a "classless society" by eliminating everyone but the peasant class. But their real goal was to get rid of the citizens who might challenge their authority and to control the world through terror.

Until that terrible pounding on our front door, I had led a charmed life. As an only child, I was surrounded by servants, a nurse, and a private tutor. Compared to most Poles in 1940, we were well off. But that was before the pounding on the door.

The moment the Russians stormed into our home, our fate was no longer in our hands. One moment we were free, the next moment we were prisoners of the Russian police. My parents didn't know where we were being sent. But they knew there was little chance of ever returning alive.

The Wheel of Fortune Turns

Where were they taking us? I thought to myself. *What would become of our beautiful home?*

Two Russian KGB agents, accompanied by two armed soldiers, were inside our home, screaming at us to hurry. All we were allowed to take was what we could shove into two suitcases or carry in our hands. My father talked to the senior KGB officer in a calm, even voice. He asked the agent why we were being asked to leave. He wanted to know if we were under arrest, what the charges were, where we were being taken. The agent's answer was always the same.

"None of your business. Now hurry up. I'm losing my patience."

I knew my father well enough to know he was stalling for time so that we could gather up more food and clothes. He understood that the more warm clothes and canned food we could pack, the better our chances for survival. My father was very organized and methodical, and if he had more time, he would have had our suitcases packed just right. But now it was too late. When the Nazis or the communists came for you in the middle of the night, it was too late for anything but prayers.

"Don't worry, Alicia," my mother said as she quickly bundled me up in the warmest clothing she could find. "Everything is going to be all right."

My mother was a strong-willed woman, and she tried to act calm and collected as she hurried around the house grabbing at clothes and valuables to stuff in our suitcase. But from time to time I would glance in her direction and catch her crying, and I knew that she, too, was terrified at what was about to happen.

Sleigh Ride to the Train Station

The senior KGB officer ordered my father to hitch two of our horses to the soldiers' heavy sleigh. My father hesitated, protesting that the horses weren't accustomed to pulling the heavy Russian sleighs, but the impatient agent was unmoved.

"Hitch up the horses — now!" he growled.

My father pulled on his heavy winter coat and headed outside to the stable. The weather was bitterly cold, and the wind cut into exposed skin like a sharp knife. All of us wrapped wool scarves around our necks and pulled our fur caps down over our ears before heading to the sleigh.

I remember one of the agents following my father to the stable and ordering him to work faster.

"Hurry!" shouted the burly agent. "We will soon be taking you to the Ukraine, where there is everything." The Ukraine, nicknamed the "breadbasket of the Soviet Union," was located in southwest Russia, and its long, warm summers and fertile fields were perfect for growing a variety of crops.

My father spat in the snow and replied coldly, "No, you mean you will be taking us to Siberia, where there is nothing!"

"Hurry!" the agent responded. "We don't have time for small talk. We've got a long journey ahead of us."

The senior agent took the reins, while the younger one positioned himself in the rear seat. My father swung our suitcases and a bulging bag of food onto the sled, and the three of us settled in. I tugged a thick blanket over my nose and nestled between my parents as the sleigh lurched forward into the darkness.

Our two dogs, Stormy and Laleczka, trotted next to the sleigh before giving up the chase. Their lonely howls were soon drowned out by the swirling wind. I dug deeper into the covers and nestled snugly into my mother's arms as the muffled rhythm of the horses' hooves and the rocking of the sleigh lulled me into a deep sleep.

Lost Dream of Freedom

Little did I know that this was the last night that little Alicia Dabrowski would sleep the deep, undisturbed sleep of a free and innocent child. Tomorrow when I awoke, my world would be a very different place. Nothing I had ever heard or seen in the first seven years of my life had prepared me for the world I was about to enter.

As the sleigh glided toward the black abyss of communism, I didn't truly understand the concept of freedom. How could I? I was too young, too sheltered, and too inexperienced to wrap my arms around freedom and hold it close, like I could hold my mother. But before another year had passed, I would learn lessons about freedom that most people 10 times my age had never learned. And I made an oath as a child that the only thing that could prevent me from living a life of freedom was death.

The wind swallowed up my mother's soft voice as the sleigh floated over the snow into the cold, black night.

"Sleep while you can, little Alicia.

Sleep, my innocent angel.

Sleep. Please sleep."

2

Train of Terror

"*Look, Mamma, a train!*" I shouted as our sleigh pulled into a small, isolated train station.

Gesturing toward the long, black train, the guard in the rear of the sleigh grunted, "There is your train. It will be taking you east."

My parents' worst fears were confirmed. We had traveled north all night and now we were heading into the heart of the Soviet Union. Our final destination was a frozen nightmare called Siberia.

The train station was packed. Men, women, and children were standing shoulder to shoulder, backs turned to a hard wind from the north. My parents recognized many of the passengers and their families. Dozens of burly Russian soldiers herded the crowd onto the train. We squeezed into a corner seat and hugged each other to stay warm.

Once we were settled in, I started to notice that this train wasn't like the other trains I had traveled on. The other trains had roomy private compartments and thick padded seats covered in velvet, with curtains to match. This train had hard wood benches and bare windows, and it was so crowded that half the passengers had to stand in the aisles.

The other trains were bright and warm, and smiling conductors stopped to greet you. This train was dark and cold, and hard-eyed soldiers stood at attention at each end of the aisle. Little did I know at the time that this train was luxurious compared to the ones we would ride in the days ahead.

"Verby! Next stop, Verby!" shouted one of the soldiers. Black smoke billowed from the smokestack as our train chugged into the vast whiteness.

Three Days in Verby

Shortly after arriving in Verby, we were told that the next train would arrive in a day or two. My parents and I pushed our way inside the packed station house and staked out a couple of square feet on the floor as our temporary living quarters.

One day passed. Two days. Three days. Still no train. We could see the Russian soldiers slurping hot soup and gobbling down thick slices of bread, but they didn't make any food available to the prisoners. My family was more fortunate than most because the agents gave us enough time to gather up a big bag of food. But many of the prisoners were arrested with just the clothes on their back, which meant they hadn't eaten in five days. The hungriest people cried at first, but as they became weaker and weaker, they retreated into silence, too exhausted and defeated to make a sound.

At the end of the third day, a thin stream of black smoke cracked the endless gray horizon. Our train was coming. The prisoners staggered to their feet, grabbed their belongings, and rushed out to greet the train. Hope surged through the noisy crowd. Surely the train would be stocked with food. Surely the passenger cars would be warm. But hope turned into shock and despair when the train pulled into the station.

From Bad to Worse

This was no passenger train — it was a black locomotive pulling a long caravan of empty boxcars! Some of the prisoners turned to go back into the station house, assuming that a passenger train was coming later in the day. But the soldiers lowered their rifles and pressed the confused prisoners toward the open boxcars. This was our mode of transportation to the Soviet Union — boxcars!

The boxcars were small by today's standards, perhaps 10 feet wide by 20 feet long. In the center of each boxcar was a squat, cast-iron stove with a stovepipe chimney jutting through the roof.

My father motioned for us to enter one of the boxcars early so that we could claim a corner space. As we dragged our belongings across the rough-cut wood floor, my mother steered me around an uneven hole cut in the floorboards. I would later learn that this hole served an invaluable purpose. It was the community toilet.

Cold-eyed soldiers forced 30 to 40 prisoners into each boxcar before the doors were slammed shut and locked. The only light came from the hole in the floor and the dancing flame in the pot-bellied stove. The rest of the space was as black as the inside of a tomb. Once again I heard the chugging engine and felt the slow pull of the train as it moved us closer to our destination.

The train swayed and creaked steadily eastward. It was hard to tell day from night in our black cabin, so I couldn't tell you how many days we traveled before we heard the brakes grinding to a stop.

Changing Trains at the Border

We had arrived at Zdolbunow, the last station on the border be-tween Russia and Poland. A Soviet official informed us that the railroad tracks on the Russian side of the border were too wide for our train, which meant we had to wait until a Russian train arrived at the station.

We were forced to remain in our boxcars for five days, while fierce February snow storms rocked the boxcars and packaged the black train into a long, thick wall of ice and snow. Once a day the soldiers released two men from each boxcar to fetch coal and water. Occasionally new prisoners were ordered into our car. More often, the captives who had died during the night were tossed off the boxcar and left face down in a snowdrift.

I huddled between my parents for warmth and protection, but they could no longer shield me from the cold, hard realities of war. The elderly and the infants were the first to freeze or starve to death, and two or three times a day we'd hear the soulful shriek of a parent who lost a child in the night. To protect myself, I snuggled closer and closer to my parents and avoided looking at the children who were pale or shivering, fearing that death would come for me next.

As the days passed, word spread throughout the neighboring villages that a freight train hauling Polish prisoners had broken down at the border. We could hear the voices of local villages calling out the names of missing relatives.

"Have you seen Jan Zabolski?"

"Where is the Szczenkowski family?"

"Please, help me find my son!"

One day when my father and another prisoner were returning to our boxcar with a load of coal and water, a young mother in the crowd of spectators caught a glimpse of her three young children.

"My babies! My babies!" she cried hysterically. "Mother will come get you now!" She ran to the nearest guard and begged him to release her children.

The guard stared straight ahead without a reply.

"Well, then," she cried. "Let me get on the train with them. I'll do anything you say. Just let me take care of my babies."

The guard stared straight ahead as if the woman did not exist.

"Please, please, let me go to my children," she pleaded.

The guard turned his head away in silence.

In desperation, the young mother fell to her knees and wrapped her thin arms around the soldier's thick legs. "Give them to me, please!" she whimpered. "Give me my children."

The guard remained silent. He drew back a tear-stained boot and kicked the unsuspecting woman squarely in the jaw. Dazed, she lunged backward and crawled away from the soldier. We watched helplessly as she disappeared into the stunned crowd.

Answered Prayers

My father continued to ration out small pieces of bread to mother and me. I wasn't aware at the time that our food supply was almost gone, but I would learn later that while I slept, my parents were praying that somehow, someway, God would deliver food to us. Miraculously, their prayers were answered the same day the Russian train pulled into the station. As the guards were marching the prisoners from our freight train to the waiting Russian train, we heard a deep, booming voice calling out to my parents.

"Joseph! Janina! Over here. Here I am, over here!"

We turned to see my mother's brother, Wicek, jumping up and down, waving his arms. Trapped in a crowd penned in behind an iron fence, Wicek couldn't reach us.

"Joseph," he shouted over the crowd. "Take this!" Wicek held a small bag above his head and encouraged the people in front of him to pass it hand over hand until my father could reach through the fence and grab it.

"Thank you, Wicek," my father shouted back. "And may God bless!"

Inside the bag were several loaves of rich, dark bread, thick slices of bacon, and an assortment of dried fruit. In the days to come this gift would make the difference between survival and starvation.

Shipped Like Livestock

As we moved closer to the Russian train, I could see my father's expression darken. Suddenly he stopped, staring at the train in disbelief.

We expected the Russian train would be a boxcar, much like the one we left behind. If only we were so lucky.

Our latest mode of transportation was an aging cattle car!

The sides of the cattle cars were made of thick boards separated by gaps two to three inches wide. As the doors flew open, we were greeted by the pungent smell of livestock and cow manure. The guards ordered us in, and we tripped over the warped floorboards as we made our way through the dark car. Pressing our faces against the wood slats, we could see a vast, endless plain of snow stretching to the horizon. The light filtered in, revealing a pot-bellied stove, a hole in the floor, and rows of rough-hewn wood bunks nailed to the walls.

Years later I realized that the cattle cars were as symbolic as they were functional, both for the prisoners and the communist party. The goal of the communists was to stomp out all expressions of individuality. The state was the end-all and be-all in communism, not the individual. The state wouldn't allow for individual differences anymore than a huge cattle farmer would allow a cow to drift apart from his herd. To the Soviets, we Poles were less than livestock.

Survival of the Fittest

The Russian cattle train carrying my family and thousands of Polish citizens chugged away from the station and headed north toward Siberia. We traveled for 30 days, stopping only occasionally to take on water and coal. When we started our trip, our car was packed with 40 men, women, and children. By the time we arrived a month later at our destination in Kotlas, a large town in southern Siberia more than 1,000 miles from the Polish border, only the strongest people in our cattle car had survived. Thanks to my Uncle Wicek's gift of food, my parents and I were among the survivors.

The last leg of our trip was tedious, to say the least. To pass the time, the prisoners sang Polish folk songs and told stories. But mostly we stared through the sideboard gaps in numbed silence. The open slats made the trip much colder, of course, but ironically, the open ventilation was also a blessing in disguise because we desperately needed the fresh air. The smell of unwashed bodies, human vomit, and feces was overwhelming. Even with the constant airflow, we were forced to take shallow breaths through our mouths to prevent nausea.

Real-Life Lessons

As miserable minutes turned into hours ... then days ... then weeks, I could feel my childhood slowly wither and die, like a cherry blossom caught in a late frost. Life was no longer about lighthearted laughter and carefree sleigh rides on moonlit nights. Life was about survival, plain and simple. At the tender age of seven, when I should have been playing with dolls, I was learning real-life lessons in survival and freedom.

I remember, for example, that one of the unspoken rules during our deportation was to take care of your own. Each family fed its own, and no one was obligated to share with outsiders. The prisoners intuitively understood this rule and honored it.

Occasionally, hunger and desperation would compel a prisoner to beg food. One day an emaciated woman crawled over to my father. Grabbing his wrist in her bony fingers she pleaded, "Please, give me some of your food. I'm so hungry."

My father turned away without a word, coldly ignoring the woman's pitiful pleas. Previously she had begged for scraps for her young son, but he'd recently lapsed into a coma, and it was only a matter of hours before he was dead. All she could do now was save herself.

My father was a generous man by nature, and I know it hurt him deeply to turn his back on suffering. But I was beginning to understand that by giving food to strangers, he could unwittingly hasten the death of his wife or daughter. So he ignored her pitiful pleas until she crawled away, mumbling incoherently. It was a brutal lesson in self-reliance that I never forgot.

The Cold Heart of Communism

Perhaps the most chilling lesson I learned happened near the end of our 30-day journey to Siberia. One morning the train rumbled to a stop, shaking the prisoners from their sleep. A thick-shouldered Russian guard opened the door to our car and ordered my father to carry coal. No sooner had he jumped to the ground when we heard a blood-curdling scream from inside the cattle car. A young father was kneeling on the floor next to a bunk, his face contorted in anguish.

"They're dead, all three! Oh, my God," he cried over and over, hovering over a bunk where his three dead children lay. He rocked and moaned while the other passengers stared in silence. I drew closer to my mother, and I could feel her hold me tighter.

Burying his nose and mouth into a heavy handkerchief to block the smell, the soldier hopped aboard the cattle car. He kicked prisoners out of his way until he reached the grieving father. Waving his arms, the soldier spat out orders in Russian. The grieving father didn't speak Russian, so he stared blankly at the soldier. The red-faced soldier kept barking orders in Russian until the young man struggled to his feet, screaming, "You killed my wife. Now you killed my children."

The soldier gripped his rifle in front of him like a shield and retorted, "Get moving, imbecile."

"Go back to hell where you came from!" the young Pole shrieked. "You are vermin!" The frail father lunged at the guard, who moved quickly to one side. Suddenly the guard swung the rifle butt with vicious force into the young man's skull. Blood gushed from the wound, spraying the cattle car and several prisoners. The Pole crumpled to the floor.

Cursing, the burly Russian positioned his rifle strap over his shoulder, lifted the victim from the floor like a sack of flour, and tossed him off the train. The young father's twisted body lay crumpled at the foot of a snow-laden bush as a growing halo of blood circled his head. The soldier returned to the bunk and grabbed the dead children one by one, tossing them out the door like an impatient baggage handler.

The guard turned to my father and growled, "Stop staring and get to work. Do you hear?"

"Yes," replied my father, his voice choked with rage. "I hear."

That vicious Russian guard put a face to communism. And as the dark blood of the dying Polish father spread across the white snow like black storm clouds on a clear horizon, I vowed to never forget the cold face of communism and to return its frozen gaze with the truth for as long as I lived.

The cattle car jerked to a final stop at an empty train station just outside the city of Kotlas. The guards herded us into an abandoned schoolhouse where we were ordered to stay until further notice.

We weren't sure what lay ahead of us, but we were relieved to breathe clean air and stretch our legs. Nothing could be worse, we thought, than what we'd had to endure during the last month.

We were wrong. The worst was yet to come.

3
Arriving at a "Workers' Paradise"

"*Wake up! Come with us!*"
My father blinked and turned his head from the bright glare of a flashlight as a vice-like grip squeezed his shoulder and shook him from a deep sleep.

Two KGB agents marched him to a storehouse next to the schoolhouse. "Are you Joseph Dabrowski?" the gruff senior agent asked as my father entered a large storage room that had been hastily converted to a KGB office.

"Yes," my father replied softly.

"Sign these papers at once," the senior agent commanded, pointing toward the papers on his desk.

My father knew he had no choice but to sign the papers. It was common knowledge that any prisoners who failed to follow orders were promptly marched outside and shot through the back of the head.

My father thumbed through the papers before scribbling his signature on the last page. The document could have been a confession that Joseph Dabrowski was operating as a spy. Or it could have confirmed that Joseph Dabrowski had worked as a capitalist collaborator. It really didn't matter what the document said. My father was powerless to do anything but sign it and pray that, by "confessing," his life would be spared for another day ... another week ... or another month.

The guards marched my father back to the schoolhouse, where they repeated the same routine with another prisoner. My father reassured my mother and me that everything was fine before delving into a sack of household items that mother had hastily "packed" in our last few minutes at home. He pulled a few items from the sack and started to work his way around the perimeter of the room, stopping to barter with fellow prisoners.

By nightfall my father had returned to our bunk. Smiling broadly, he presented my mother with three loaves of dark brown bread, for which he had traded a wool blanket. It was enough food to keep us alive for another week.

Sleigh Ride to Mala Jeluga

"One family to a sleigh," barked the Russian guard. "Hurry along!"

We had been sequestered in the schoolhouse in Kotlas for four days, and all of the prisoners were grateful for the shelter from the cold. But because the "indoor plumbing" consisted of several holes cut in the wood floor, the stench of human waste and unwashed bodies had become so overpowering we were relieved when the Russians told us to pack our things for a sleigh ride.

Our caravan of sleighs traveled north on a frozen river that cut through a thick Siberian forest. We were more than 1,000 miles from our hometown in Poland, and most of those miles were due north. As best we could figure, it was early in April when we departed the schoolhouse in Kotlas for our final destination, Mala Jeluga, a slave-labor camp named after a nearby river.

As we made our way north, most of Europe was enjoying an early spring. Back home the snow was melting and green buds were popping out on the trees in our front yard. But spring wouldn't visit Siberia for several more months, and the temperature was well below freezing as our sleighs glided around the gentle river bends. We slumped down in our seats and pulled the blankets over our noses to protect ourselves from the raw arctic wind.

My mother and me after our reunion in Africa. I was 9.

Alicia Gilewicz

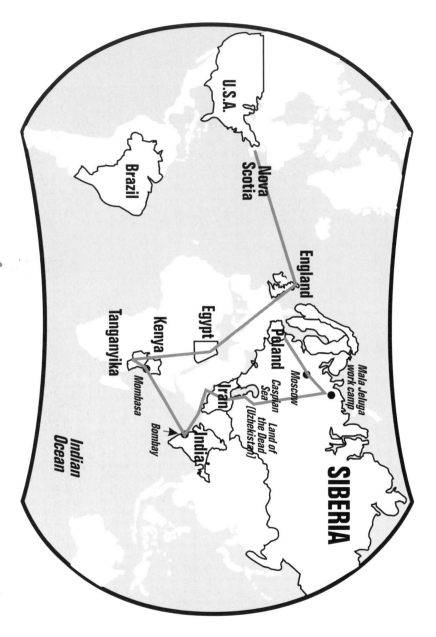

World map showing our travels beginning in Poland, 1940.

A boxcar used to transport Jews to concentration camps, similar in size to the ones used to transport us from Poland to Siberia.

My mother and me the day we arrived in Pahlevi, Iran. Notice I was wearing my underwear, my only clothing for several months. My mother was in her Polish army uniform.

My mother and me (third and fourth from left) *posing with fellow refugees in front of our tukulas at the Polish settlement in Africa.*

Children sitting atop a recently killed elephant (I'm sitting in the center). *Woman is cutting the flank into elephant steaks.*

Tall, graceful members of the Masai tribe.

My mother hiking in Kenya. Behind her is the highest mountain in Africa, Mt. Kilimanjaro.

Alicia Gilewicz

*Hank standing in front
of his brownstone apart-
ment in Brooklyn.
Hank was 10.*

*17-year-old Hank
standing in Watertown,
Wisconsin, where he
visited his older sister.*

Our wedding day, May 24, 1958.

I graduated from the University of Bridgeport, a dream come true. It was 1958.

Senator Jesse Helms flanked by his wife, Dot, (on left) and me, in 1973.

Hank and I met Ronald and Nancy Reagan during the 1980 presidential campaign.

Hank, Mark, and me with President George Bush.

Hank and me with Dick DeVos, President of the Amway Corporation, and his wife Betsy.

I had the honor of sharing a stage with one of my heroes, Dr. Norman Vincent Peale, at a weekend function in Portland, OR.

Hank and me with General Norman Schwarzkopf.

A packed arena at a major function in Poland.

Photo of a boys' home we sponsor just outside Zawichost, Poland.

A family portrait while enjoying a Caribbean cruise in the spring of 1997. Mark is on my right. Michael stands next to his father.

Mark standing with his friend Billy Childers next to Senator Jesse Helms on the steps of the Capitol. Mark and Billy worked as interns in Washington, DC, for several months during the Bush Administration.

Mark speaking at a rally in mainland, China, 1996.

Mark posing with Doug DeVos, Senior Vice President and Managing Director of North America for the Amway Corporation, 1995, at the Georgia Dome in Atlanta.

Hank and me with some of our Hong Kong distributors during an event in Hong Kong, 1995.

I'm enjoying a meal during one of our visits to Hong Kong.

Like a Crown of Thorns

After three days the sleighs slowed to a stop in a small clearing surrounded by massive pine trees. Peering over the top of my blanket, I could see two weathered wood buildings surrounded by a tall barbed wire fence.

"The barbed wire circles the camp like a crown of thorns," my mother whispered in the direction of my father. He turned to meet my mother's gaze and reached across me to pat her hand. This was Mala Jeluga, my home for the next two years.

The guards marched us into our barracks. The walls were lined with rows of narrow wood bunks. Several of the prisoners groaned as they entered the barracks, remarking that the barracks weren't much bigger or more accommodating than the boxcars they had traveled in.

"You ingrates," scolded a short, stocky guard in flawless Polish. "You don't know how fortunate you are to live in these buildings. Our first guests weren't so fortunate. By day they cut the timber to build these barracks. At night they slept in ditches — ditches that soon became their graves! You see, the barracks you are standing in were built during the winter. None of the laborers survived. Not one! You are very fortunate, indeed!"

The Hypocrisy of Communism

The Mala Jeluga labor camp was the communists' idea of a workers' paradise. In one sense they were right. Mala Jeluga was truly a classless society for us prisoners — we were all equally miserable!

At the time I was too young and inexperienced to understand the real motivation behind communism. The founders of communism insisted their movement was about justice for all the workers who had been exploited by capitalists.

But the older I got, the more I realized that the real motivation behind communism was envy. The communists hated the thought that some people could accumulate more wealth than others by working harder ... by saving more ... by making sacrifices ... by being better prepared ... by being smarter.

According to the communists' party line, the purpose of the revolution was to level the playing field by redistributing wealth from the upper and middle classes to the lower class. But in truth, the party leaders made sure that never happened by keeping all the spoils for themselves! Lenin and Stalin talked a good game, but don't think for a second that they lived like the rank and file worker in the Soviet Union. Stalin owned seven Rolls Royces during his lifetime. Lenin outdid him — he owned nine!

The communists' strategy of starving innocent people to death in forced labor camps wasn't about building a Utopian society. It was about acquiring power through terror, and no amount of slanted propaganda and clever slogans could disguise the truth for very long.

First Night

That first night, my parents and I huddled together on our bunk, which was nothing more than two narrow boards placed side by side. When most children my age were wondering what gifts they would receive on their birthdays, I wondered, "Will I have to stay here for the rest of my life?"

When most children were wondering if they could have a friend over for the afternoon, I wondered, "Will I ever live to see our home in Dubno?"

When most children were wondering what they were having for dessert after dinner, I wondered, "Will my parents get sick and die, like so many of the others?"

I wish I could forget what I saw and lived through in Siberia, but that's impossible. We took better care of our livestock back home than our captors took care of us. The barracks were filled with bugs and the beds were full of lice. The smell was like living in an outhouse. Our feet and hands ached constantly from the cold, and our heads and stomachs ached constantly from hunger.

I still remember the prisoners who wrapped their feet in rags because their only pair of shoes had worn out. Often, as they marched into the woods, they left their bloody red footprints in the white Siberian snow. Many nights when I would get up to go to the bathroom, I saw the guards carrying out the prisoners who had died during the night.

This was communism in action. This was their idea of creating a workers' paradise. In reality, this was a frozen hell surrounded by a "crown of thorns." My only comfort was that the three of us were still together.

"One day we will all be free. This will only be a memory," my mother mumbled as we stowed our diminishing supply of food and clothing under our warped, splintered bunk. Still on her knees, she bowed her head. "Dear Father ..." she started.

But her words were strangled by a rush of tears.

4
No Work, No food

The unwritten slogan for the Mala Jeluga labor camp was *"Kak nie rabotajesz tak nie kuszasz"*. — "If you do not work, you do not eat." This rule was the camp mandate, and it applied to men, women, and children alike.

This rule was, of course, a death sentence for many prisoners. The ones who were too sick, too old, or too young to work died. The guards carried the cadavers outside during the night and rolled them down the banks of the Mala Jeluga River like fresh cut logs.

We weren't there a week before the prisoners settled into the dreary work routine. Six days a week we rose at daybreak and trudged into the arctic forests to cut timber in subzero temperatures. The men's job was to cut down the trees and remove the big branches. The women and children stripped away the small branches and then stacked and burned them. Everyone helped build the huge rafts that the guards would use to carry the logs downstream to the saw mills.

Our spirits sank the lowest when we awakened to a fresh

snowfall, for it meant we had to clear new paths through the snowbanks with the only tools available to us — our bodies. We would march to the worksite in single file, each person taking his turn as the leader, shoveling the snow to the side with his arms and legs. On the occasions when we would have to fight our way through five-foot-high drifts, we were exhausted by the time we reached the worksite — yet we faced nine more hours of back-breaking labor.

For 10 hours of hard labor under brutal conditions, each prisoner was paid two rubles per week, which enabled my family to purchase a couple loaves of bread and three bowls of soup each day from the "camp cafeteria." The thin, gray soup was made from low-grade oats, salt, and water. We might get lucky and discover a fish head floating in our soup on the days the guards went fishing. These were occasions for celebration.

My mother was only five feet tall and weighed less than 100 pounds, so the logging work was especially exhausting for her. Her warmest clothing was a ski outfit that barely held out the sharp arctic winds. Still, she would not allow my father to use our meager wages to buy warmer clothes from our fellow prisoners. Nor would she allow him to trade the good leather shoes he had bought from a fellow prisoner during our brief stay in Kotlas. The shoes didn't fit my father, but my parents knew they had great bargaining potential.

One day I suggested to my mother that she trade the large piece of silk which lay folded in the bottom of our suitcase for a warmer coat. Because so many prisoners were dying, there was always used clothing available for trade. But mother insisted she was saving the silk for a special occasion. How could I have known at the time that two years later, that small piece of fabric would save our lives?

Most mornings I got up very early to stand in the soup line so my parents could sleep a little longer. If the soup line was too long, I'd maneuver my way to the front of the line and get our food before we headed out to the forest.

For a seven-year old, I was exceptionally responsible. But one morning I overslept. Realizing my mistake, I grabbed my bowl and darted over to the kitchen, praying there was enough soup left for my family. Fortunately, there was! I smiled as the woman ladled the thin soup into my bowl, and I turned and hurried back to the barracks as fast as I could go.

Suddenly, I tripped and fell! I watched helplessly as the warm, gray liquid flew out of the bowl, forming a shallow, steaming depression as it melted into the snow. I fell to my knees and wept as my empty stomach tightened. I ran back to the barracks in tears, ashamed that I had let my parents down. My carelessness meant we would go without food until dinner.

As the weeks melted into months, we adjusted as best we could to the daily routine of heavy labor, little food, and miserable living conditions. Simple pleasures that we took for granted a few short months ago, like daily baths and clean sheets and privacy in the bathroom, had long since disappeared. The Soviets did, however, allow the prisoners to receive censored letters from relatives and friends back home, and opening a letter was greeted enthusiastically, for it meant that someone outside the camp knew we were alive and not forgotten.

Off to School

One afternoon when we returned to our barracks we noticed an announcement from the commandant pinned to the bulletin board. The commandant had decided to allow the children to attend school in the village. My parents immediately saw the announcement for what it was — a propaganda move on the part of the Soviets, who would use the gesture as a public relations ploy to show the rest of the world how fair and humane they were toward their captives. My parents didn't appreciate allowing their only child to be used as a pawn in the game of international politics, but they agreed that any school was better than no school. I was enrolled in the first grade.

Each morning when my mother and father went to the forest, I walked for over a mile alone through the wolf-infested woods and across a cemetery to a little one-room schoolhouse. I had received private tutoring back in Dubno, but I was never taught Russian, which meant, of course, that I was far behind the other children. But I was a quick learner, and within a short time, I was receiving high marks.

Word got back to the commandant that little Alicia Dabrowski was performing exceptionally well at the local school.

He was so pleased that he called my father into his office.

"Dabrowski," the commandant said calmly, "there is something you must know."

"Yes, sir," my father replied anxiously.

"As you know, Dabrowski, we are aware of everything that happens at Mala Jeluga. And we have been keeping a close watch on your daughter, Alicia."

"Alicia?" my father stammered. "What has she done?"

The commandant smiled and replied, "Your daughter, it seems, has made remarkable progress in her studies. The teacher says Alicia is one of her best pupils!"

My father's body uncoiled with relief. "Thank you," he beamed. "I'm very pleased to hear that."

"Yes," continued the commandant, "your daughter is an achiever. She will make outstanding contributions to the communist way of life. You should be very proud. If she keeps progressing at this pace, we might want to send her away to another school."

It was a wonderful compliment, but my father cringed at the idea of me being sent away from my mother and him. To make matters worse, he was concerned that his only child was being brainwashed into becoming a little communist!

His worries were groundless, of course. Even though I was only a child, I had learned the hard way that action speaks louder than words. I'd experienced firsthand the ugly face of communism, and their pretty slogans didn't fool me at all. I recited the party line at school with the best of them. But in my heart, I was as free as the wind over our wheat field back home in Poland. And nothing the communists could say or do would ever change that!

With the onset of summer, the snowdrifts melted, turning our worksite into a swamp. Black flies and mosquitoes attacked us relentlessly, but they were little more than a nuisance compared to the dreaded *pluskwa*, tick-like creatures that hid under tree bark and attached themselves to the clothing of the unsuspecting prisoners. At night the insidious blood-sucking pluskwa embedded in our bunks would feast on our flesh as we slept. We would awake to red, painful bites all over our bodies, and as we tossed on our filthy clothing and headed back into the forest, we dreaded the hungry insects that were waiting for us.

We watched helplessly as the camp slowly deteriorated in the thick, muggy summer air. Rotted by mildew, our threadbare clothing started to disintegrate. Everything, and everybody, was continually wet and clammy, and when the guards locked up our barracks for the night, we suffocated from the humid stench in the unventilated barracks.

My parents were religious, and I'm convinced their unwavering faith was the single biggest reason we survived our constant hardships. Sometimes they would compare our misery with the trials of Job, whose faith in God remained strong despite years of suffering and misery.

Our trials and tribulations were a long way from over at this point, however, for in late July, the Dabrowski family was about to face its greatest crisis to date. My mother decided to break one of the cardinal rules of the Mala Jeluga slave-labor camp.

My mother refused to work!

5
Solitary Confinement

"**J**anina, are you sure you don't want to report to work?" my father asked as we shared our evening meal of soup and bread. My mother leaned forward and placed a hand on his arm before answering.

"Yes, I'm sure."

"But do you know what punishment they have in mind?"

"No, I don't," my mother sighed, "but I do know that working in the swamp every day is just as dangerous to my health as any punishment they could think up. I can't go on like this, Joseph. I must take a stand."

"Even at the risk of losing your life?" my father asked solemnly.

"I will lose my life if I keep going into that swamp. This is my only chance of survival," my mother replied.

My father nodded his head, resigned to the fact that sometime during the next few days, his wife would be led away by the guards to an unknown fate. Countless prisoners had been executed for refusing an order. He could only bow his head and pray that his wife would be an exception.

True to her word, my mother stayed in the barracks while the rest of the prisoners marched off to work. By mid-morning two guards stomped into her barracks and escorted my mother to the commandant's office. My mother stared straight ahead in silence as the commandant angrily paced back and forth in front of her.

"Surely you are aware, Janina, that your behavior cannot be tolerated."

The commandant planted himself directly in front of my mother, placing his face inches from her and staring directly into her eyes.

"Insubordination is a very serious offense. Very serious. You are mocking the revolution, Janina. But if you will agree to go back to work, we'll forget about this incident."

Straightening herself to her full height, my mother met the commandant's menacing stare.

"I understand your position," she replied evenly. "But I simply cannot agree to continue working in that swamp."

"Think it over, Janina. If you do not work tomorrow, you will be punished. Think long and hard before you make a decision you'll certainly regret!"

The conversation with the commandant failed to persuade my mother to change her mind. She refused to report to work again the next morning. While the rest of the prisoners marched off to the swamp, my mother sat on her bunk bed, mending our tattered clothing and praying silently to herself. Two Russian soldiers burst into the barracks before noon and dragged my mother off to jail in Us Zaruba, a small peasant village near our camp.

"May I take some things with me?" she asked, hoping they would allow her to take along some food and blankets.

"No," shouted a tall soldier impatiently. "You are to come as you stand."

"How long will I be away?" my mother asked.

"As long as it takes," the second soldier replied, *"to break your spirit!"*

The Prison in Us Zaruba

The soldiers marched my mother over rocky countryside for six miles to the prison in Us Zaruba. As my mother entered the compound, her worst fears were confirmed. It was not so much a prison as a fenced stockyard containing rows of tiny wood cubicles that resembled outhouses. She was ushered into a tiny cell that stunk of stale human sweat and excrement. When the door slammed shut, my mother was enveloped in darkness. She shuffled across the dirt floor to her "bed," a splintered plank lying on the floor next to the back wall.

"Good thing I'm short," my mother thought to herself as she laid down on the rotting plank. Only five feet tall, she could barely extend her legs fully without hitting a side wall. The room was completely black except for slivers of light that filtered in through the cracks between the warped sideboards.

On her seventh day of imprisonment, my mother resigned herself to death. She had not eaten since her last morning at Mala Jeluga, and as she lay shivering on the splintered plank in her black cell, she could feel the small, slimy *pluskwa* crawling into her eyes, nose, and ears. She was too weak to raise her arms to brush them away. She received a small bowl of water each morning, but she thought the daily visit by a guard was a thinly disguised way to discover if she had died during the night.

Visits from an Angel

My mother was certain she would not have lasted seven days if it hadn't been for several nighttime visits by a mysterious woman. The first visit occurred on the third night of imprisonment. Too hungry and sick to sleep, my mother was squatting on her bench, listening to the mice scurrying across the dirt floor.

Suddenly she heard a rustling sound brushing against the rear wall of her cell. My mother thought it was a wild animal scavenging for food, when a soft voice whispered, *"Here, eat this!"*

Following the sound of the voice, my mother inched her hands down the bench until she found a small hole gouged out of a rotting side board. She reached down and pulled a cool, firm object through the opening. It was a potato.

Two nights later, as my mother lay sick from hunger and a high fever, she heard the familiar rustling sound outside her cell. *"Courage,"* a voice as soft as a breeze whispered. Slowly, my mother dragged her aching limbs to the crack in the wall and pulled another small potato through the opening.

By the seventh day of solitary confinement, my mother started to hallucinate. Her imagination flashed back and forth from her dank cell to her freshly dug grave. The tiny *pluskwa* covered her entire body, but mercifully, her hunger had driven all of the sensation from her body, so she could no longer feel the pain of their stings.

"Our Father, who art in Heaven," she prayed in a hoarse whisper, "hallowed be Thy name. Thy kingdom come, Thy will be done, on earth, as it is in Heaven."

She repeated the Lord's Prayer over and over, taking comfort in the words and the rhythm. Finally she fell into a deep, feverish sleep.

"Janina. Wake up, Janina. You must wake up!"

A woman's urgent voice roused my mother from her semiconscious state. She forced open her swollen eyelids and tried to focus on the blurry silhouette bending over her bunk. My mother tried her best to speak, but she could barely force her cracked bleeding lips open wide enough to form words.

"Don't try to speak now," the woman said soothingly. "I'm a doctor, and I'm here to help you," she continued as she bathed mother's wounds with a cool antiseptic. "Someone from the prison came by my office and told me to come over right away, before it was too late. Hold on, dear, and I promise to get you out of this hell-hole tomorrow."

"I promise I'll be alive when you return," my mother rasped as the cell door slammed shut behind the doctor. "I promise."

"Mother! What have they done to you?" I shrieked, running toward my mother as she crawled to the edge of the Mala Jeluga compound. I wept as I helped my pale, emaciated mother to her feet. My father swept my mother up in his arms and carried her back to the barracks, where he bathed her oozing sores and lovingly fed her soup and bread.

"Rest, my darling," my father urged. "We want you to get well as soon as possible."

"I love you both," my mother whispered. "Tears were welling up in her eyes as she struggled to talk through her cracked lips. "And, Joseph," she smiled painfully, "they didn't break my spirit."

Organizing a School for Children

Amazingly, my mother's spirit was stronger than ever after her return from prison. Once she regained her strength, she returned to work, but not in the swamp. The commandant assigned my mother the job of retrieving the daily mail from a post office two and one-half miles away and returning to the camp before noon. This schedule gave my mother a lot of free time during the afternoons, and she decided to put that time to good use.

My mother had long observed that the religious and educational needs of the children in the camp had been neglected since their arrest nearly a year ago. She soon rallied the parents in the barracks behind her, and with their support, she organized classes for the children after supper. Every evening many of the children gathered around my mother for lessons in reading and writing in Polish. At the end of each class, my mother would lead the children in prayer. One evening two burly guards burst into our barracks just as the children were kneeling during prayer.

"You crazy devils! What are you doing?" shouted one of the guards in Russian.

The startled children turned and looked to my mother for guidance. Still kneeling, she calmly signaled to the children to finish their prayers and then rose to face the guards.

"We are worshiping God," my mother replied coolly in the guard's native language. *"Would you care to join us?"*

The guards replied with a spray of obscenities, glaring menacingly at my mother before stomping out the door. My mother took a deep breath, preparing herself emotionally for what was about to happen.

"Here we go again!" the commandant thundered. "Always the trouble-maker, Dabrowski. Always the ringleader. Enough! You will cease your trouble making immediately!"

My mother felt her shoulders sagging from the scolding, but forced herself to straighten her posture and meet the commandant's stare.

"If you ignore my demand this time, Janina, you will be sent away again," the commandant hissed through clenched teeth. "And this time, I promise you, you won't be coming back!"

My mother walked out of the commandant's office with her shoulders back and her chin held high. It was only after she turned the corner of the barracks that her shoulders slumped in soul-shattering disappointment.

The Second Winter in Mala Jeluga

The second winter brought more sickness and death to the prisoners at Mala Jeluga, but luckily, everyone in the Dabrowski family survived. My father had been promoted to the leader of the workers' brigade, enabling us to buy more food from the camp kitchen and more warm clothing from the survivors of deceased prisoners.

My parents and I would sometimes reminisce about the "good old days" that now seemed so long ago. Occasionally we would dream of a future time when we would be free once again, but, realistically, the dream of freedom seemed as remote and frozen as our arctic prison. Mostly we lived in the present, surviving from one meal to the next, grateful to wake up to our misery in the morning because most likely, death had claimed a fellow prisoner during the night.

Winter surrendered to a late spring. The prisoners greeted the month of June with mixed emotions — we loved the warm sun on our faces, but hated working in the insect-ridden swamp. After 16 months of captivity, it seemed like our monotonous daily routine would go on forever.

How many more springs would we witness the frozen footprints of winter dissolve into mud? Would the cold hands of communism ever release its grip from our throats, so that we could breathe freely once again? Could my parents fight off another ambush of winter?

I didn't dwell on these questions, for fear I couldn't bear the answer.

6

Dawn of Freedom

I t was just a matter of time before the pact between Hitler and Stalin would unravel, for both men were scheming, ruthless dictators who ordered the cold-blooded murder of millions of their own countrymen.

Hitler quickly gained the upper hand, ordering the German army to invade the Soviet Union on June 22, 1941. Within days of the surprise attack, Poland and the Soviet Union opened negotiations to become unlikely allies in a life-and-death struggle against the German war machine. Within a month of the German invasion, Poland entered into an uneasy alliance with its centuries-old enemy, Russia.

The news of the new Polish-Soviet alliance soon reached the Mala Jeluga labor camp. Although the alliance meant that the prisoners and the guards were technically fighting on the same side now, little changed in the day-to-day workings of the camp. In fact, the communists reduced our food rations and increased our work loads in order to stockpile supplies in anticipation of the shortages that lay ahead.

Emboldened by Freedom

We prisoners endured our increased hardships with a renewed sense of optimism, for we knew our release could come at any moment. The sweet dream of freedom swept into our barracks like a scented breeze, and my parents and I talked incessantly about returning to our home.

In September the camp commander began calling prisoners into his office, and they quickly returned waiving their freedom papers. Day after day the sparse barracks rang with shouting and laughter as one family after the other celebrated their long-awaited freedom papers.

"Papa, are we leaving? Are we going home?" I asked breathlessly when my father entered the barracks brandishing our papers.

"Yes, dear Alicia. We're leaving. We're free!" my father shouted as he hoisted me onto his shoulders and then playfully hugged my smiling, weeping mother.

The freedom celebrations didn't last long, however, as families wrestled with the reality of what it meant to be free in Siberia, especially with the brutal winter only days away. Several of the prisoners, wearing nothing more than the rags on their backs, left the labor camp the day they received their papers. Others, like my family, chose to wait and plan their departure. A few families, lacking food and money to pay for transportation, had no choice but to stay and work for food and lodging.

My father continued to work as a supervisor in the forest through the end of September, but in October, he took a higher-paying job transporting war materials in Us Zaruba, the village where my mother had been imprisoned. By November we had saved enough to make our first move toward returning home. My father paid a farmer to take us to a supply town 25 miles outside of Mala Jeluga. We weren't sure how we were going to get back home, but at least we were moving away from the inevitable death that awaited every worker at Mala Jeluga.

We traveled southward from village to village, hitching rides on wagons, sleighs, or trucks. Because we weren't welcomed as boarders, we usually slept in barns or open fields. On December 7, 1941, when we arrived back in Kotlas, the bustling city where our train trip ended almost two years prior, I was barely eight years old. I vividly remember my parents and I walking hand in hand down the main street, grimacing and huddling closer together in silence as we passed the cold, gray train station.

Miles and Miles to Go

We were deep in the Soviet Union, more than 1,000 miles from the Polish border. All we had to our name was the clothes on our backs, a few rubles, and a suitcase containing tattered clothing, a pair of men's shoes, two yards of silk cloth, and half a loaf of stale bread. Despite our poverty, my parents and I were full of hope because we had each other, and we had our freedom — at least for the moment!

"What now, Joseph?" my mother asked as we rested on a low wall skirting a small pond near the city square.

"That depends," my father said solemnly. "If there are enough Polish citizens interested, perhaps we could travel in a group for protection." My father paced nervously back and forth as he searched for answers.

Suddenly my father raised his hand to silence our conversation and leaned forward toward the street. We could barely make out a thin warble from a slow-moving truck mounted with a loud speaker. As the truck moved steadily toward us, we were able to piece together the repeated message. "Japan has attacked Pearl Harbor! The United States has entered the war against Japan and Germany!"

My parents embraced excitedly. "With the United States on our side, we cannot lose the war to the Germans," my mother exclaimed. "We must make plans to get out of this country, Joseph. Now there is real hope for us. *Alicia ... Joseph ... there is real hope for us!*"

My parents arranged for us to sleep in a barn just outside the city. Early the next morning my father headed into Kotlas to see about organizing all the Polish refugees in the area. By the end of the day, several thousand Polish refugees pooled their money to rent an entire train of boxcars bound for southern Russia — out of Siberia forever!

All Aboard the Freedom Train

Almost two years after hundreds of Polish families were ordered off the cattle cars at the Kotlas train station, Polish families once again lined up to travel thousands of miles in rough-hewn wood boxcars. Although the mode of transportation was the same, this second trip was far different. First of all, the train was headed south, away from Siberia. Best of all, the passengers were no longer political prisoners. *We were free!*

In many ways the condition of the passengers, including the Dabrowski family, was worse on our second journey. All of us had endured two years of a near-starvation diet and long days of back-breaking labor. Food was even more scarce than before. We were covered with lice, and the body odor was gut-wrenching, for most of the passengers hadn't bathed or changed clothes in months.

Yet on this train ride we could hear occasional laughter. Now and then a passenger would flash a toothless grin. The passengers' eyes were brighter and their voices were lighter. We were riding the same boxcars as before. We were enduring the same miserable circumstances as before. Yet a bright ray of hope pierced the black veil of despair. *We were free!*

"Here we were, a trainload of human wreckage," my father would say years later when recalling the day we boarded the freedom train. "And yet when I looked around, I saw smiling faces. Why? Because we finally had something to live for. We had a reason to survive. What kept us going was the promise of freedom."

"Come on! We can get a few more in here," shouted an emaciated man in rags as he waved another family inside his boxcar. "Come on in — at least 40 people to a car. We don't take up as much room as before!" he grinned, exposing raw, red sores on his gums from scurvy.

The passengers eagerly scrambled aboard the freedom train, and one by one the gray procession of boxcars was filled with scrawny, filthy passengers standing shoulder to shoulder. We staggered and swayed as the train lurched away from the now deserted train station. My father smiled at my mother and me and pulled us closer to him.

The chain of creaking boxcars lumbered southward, snaking around the Ural Mountains and groaning loudly through joyless Russian villages and cities. At one station a few young Poles risked their lives by sneaking onto a Soviet supply train loaded with flour and stealing as many bags as they could carry. At another station we gratefully accepted delousing. The treatment didn't last long, however, for we were reinfected as soon as we re-entered the lice-infested boxcars.

Bartering for Bread

We had been traveling for several weeks when our meager food supply was gone. My parents decided that my father should barter one of our few possessions for food at the next stop.

"The silk, Janina," said my father. "Surely we can find a wealthy Russian who would love to surprise his wife with that lovely piece of silk."

"I'd rather not part with it yet," my mother protested. "It's our most valuable possession, and this isn't the time. Let's dust off those new boots of yours. I'll bet you can find a buyer for those."

Once again my mother's decision to hold onto the green silk cloth would turn out to be the best decision of her life, for that shimmering piece of cloth would later save us.

My father quickly jumped off the train at the next stop and scoured the streets for potential buyers. Within minutes he spotted a young KGB agent, and my father approached him, brandishing a shiny pair of leather boots. After several minutes of intense haggling, the young soldier gruffly issued his final offer.

"Nine loaves of bread for the shoes. Take it or leave it!"

"Wear them in good health," my father responded as he quickly counted the loaves of fresh, dark bread before hurrying back to the waiting train.

Later that evening my family and a few close friends feasted on the dense bread, and we all agreed that they had never tasted a more delicious pair of shoes!

The Soviet Union was massive, easily twice the size of the continental United States, but the vast majority of land was uninhabited. As the days turned into weeks, the endless plains of the Soviet Union engulfed the train like a lake swallowing a single raindrop. Our bread rations grew smaller and smaller, while the stops between stations grew longer and longer. And still the train rolled on relentlessly southeast toward Afghanistan until we reached Uzbekistan, a sparsely populated desert region bordered on the west by the Caspian Sea and situated several hundred miles north of Iran.

At a stopover in Sarasyja, a small oasis town, my parents learned that jobs were available for tractor drivers to work the irrigated cotton fields. My father could qualify for immediate employment, which would enable us to feed ourselves until we could save enough money to continue our journey to freedom. Desperate, my parents decided to stay and work in Uzbekistan rather than risk certain starvation by continuing to travel by train.

Although grateful to have a small income as well as a mud hut to live in, my parents were terrified at the prospect of surviving for long in Uzbekistan, a barren, desolate region the local Russians called "the land of the dead." For his daily labor, working sunup to sundown, my father received two or three small onions and a small piece of *lepioszka*, a flat, tasteless bread that looked like stale pita bread — and nothing more.

We soon realized that my father's rations were barely enough for one small child to live on, much less a family of three. The longer we lived in Uzbekistan — thousands of miles from any country that could be described as politically free — the more desperate we became. We were determined to continue our travels until we arrived in a land of freedom.

But first we had to survive in the Land of the Dead.

7

The Land of the Dead

It was easy to see why the Russians called Uzbekistan the Land of the Dead. Bloated, rotting corpses littered the countryside, and the scent of decomposing bodies clung in the air, as heavy as humidity in a tropical climate.

The only thing that prevented Uzbekistan from returning to its natural state — a merciless wind-whipped, rock-littered wasteland — was an extensive network of irrigation ditches that fed the scattered, government-run rice and cotton farms.

Even before the war, day-to-day survival was a losing struggle in Uzbekistan, but the war shortages and the communist takeover of the few productive businesses made survival nearly impossible. We did our best to supplement our diet, but food was virtually non-existent. My father received one lepioszka a day at his job, and from time to time he was able to buy two to three small onions at the market. My mother stirred two tablespoons of tasteless flour into a pan of hot water for extra "nutrition." That was our only food, and it was disappearing fast!

It's easy to take food for granted when it's all around you, as it is in our country today. But all of the inhabitants in the Land of the Dead were literally days away from starvation. Ironically, the physical symptoms of hunger weren't the biggest challenges we faced. We never got used to the gnawing, burning sensation in our stomachs, of course, but we learned to ignore it.

But we couldn't ignore the way hunger consumed every waking minute of our lives. Our thoughts were consumed by food. Our conversations centered around food. Our actions, both big and small, were directed at acquiring more food. In effect, our lives were reduced to the pursuit of food. From the moment we first awakened until the moment we fell into a restless, bone-dead sleep, our quest, our reason for living, our Holy Grail, was food. Any food. *Please, just one more morsel of food!*

In the Land of the Dead, food was more scarce than it was in the Mala Jeluga labor camp. Ironically, the three of us were among the fortunate few, for at least my father had a "paying" job. Most of the inhabitants were jobless and homeless. Some of our neighbors were so hungry they resorted to eating grass mixed with cow or camel dung — a desperate act that usually led to a protracted, painful death from intestinal diseases like cholera and dysentery. Racked by uncontrollable spasms of vomiting and defecation, the victims died from dehydration. The bodies littered the barren landscape like gray driftwood, as twisted and rigid as the fallen limbs of an ancient, dying oak tree.

By the fifth week in Uzbekistan, our situation had become hopeless. The shelves in the town market were bare. So like thousands of other human skeletons stalking the Land of the Dead, we scavenged for food, any food, drifting silently across the endless Uzbekistan wasteland like wisps of gray smoke.

During the day, while my father was at work, my mother and I would walk for miles in the cold rain picking up cotton branches to use as firewood, kicking at stones to uncover a snake or rodent that we could catch for dinner. All three of us grew weaker from hunger and cold, but the lack of nutrition finally caught up with me. I became so weak I could barely lift myself from my pallet on the dirt floor.

At one point my pulse became so weak that my mother thought I'd died.

"Dear God," my mother prayed as I lay sleeping. "There must be something we can do. Please, God, help my husband and me provide food for our sick child. Please, merciful Father, there must be something we can do. Please, let my child live!"

My Father Enlists in the Polish Army

Then one afternoon my father rushed into our mud hut bursting with excitement. "Janina! They're here! The Polish Military Committee has arrived, and they're enlisting Polish refugees into the army!"

This was an opportunity my parents had been praying for. My father had a chance to fight the hated Nazis and to receive a bigger salary and increased rations. My parents quickly agreed to a desperate plan for survival: My father would join the Polish army, but first he would arrange for the commandant of the cotton farm to interview my mother for a job. The commandant was a friend of the director of the tractor factory where my father worked, and my mother's background in horticulture could be very useful to the commandant.

"It's truly a miracle, Joseph," my mother cried. "God has heard our prayers and has blessed us with these opportunities. Alicia and I will miss you, my darling, but we will be fine. God is watching over us."

My father knelt down and hugged me, but I was so weak with exhaustion and fever that I couldn't lift my arms to hug him back. I could only cry and whisper, "I'll miss you, Papa. I'll miss you."

My father gave my mother a long tearful embrace in the doorway.

"Don't worry about me, darling," he said as he held the rations in her hands. "The army always feeds its soldiers." Then he ducked through the door and headed off to enlist.

My mother was devastated by my father's leaving, but she didn't have time to sit in a corner and feel sorry for herself. She had three days' food and a sick child to care for. Just as my father promised, my mother was interviewed by the commandant of the cotton collective and immediately hired to work in the tractor brigade. The commandant directed her to return to town to secure the proper employment papers.

The government office my mother was sent to was damp and crowded. A thick, blue haze of tobacco smoke hung in the air, and the room was silent as a tomb except for the occasional shout, "next" that echoed across the dull room.

Meeting Mrs. L

As my mother waited her turn in line, she noticed a pale, thin middle-aged woman staring at her. The woman's long neck and sharp, hooked nose exacerbated her haggard, stick-figure appearance. But her smile was warm and inviting, and she moved with grace and confidence.

"Forgive me for staring, but I couldn't help noticing you," the woman said in a refined Polish dialect as she approached my mother. "You stand out from everyone else here. You have such a sparkle in your eyes."

Blushing slightly, my mother replied, "If my eyes sparkle, it's because there is hope for survival. You see, I was afraid my daughter would starve to death, but now I have a job. I'll be able to buy food for us!"

"Wonderful," the woman said enthusiastically. "Tell me all about your child. How old is she? Where is she now?"

Before reaching the front of the line the two women had exchanged their personal stories. The woman was Mrs. Helena Laskownicka, a university-educated Polish aristocrat who had been married to a successful newspaper editor before the secret police carried them off to a labor camp, where her husband died. Hungry and alone, "Mrs. L," as she was known by her friends, was looking for a way to survive.

"Here is what I've been trying to eat," the woman sighed as she pulled a few rock-hard seeds from her apron pocket. "It's called *makuchy*. It's a waste product of cotton oil. No nutritional value at all. But I chew and think of thick slices of ham," she laughed, tossing one of the hard balls into her mouth.

"Mrs. L," my mother said thoughtfully, "neither of us has anything of value today, but I think we could be great help to each other tomorrow."

"What do you mean, dear?" Mrs. L's dark eyes flashed with excitement.

"I'll be starting work tomorrow, but my daughter doesn't have anyone to take care of her," my mother answered. "Would you watch my Alicia for me? In return, you can move in with us."

"Oh, my dear, You're a godsend. Of course I'll take care of your little girl. The three of us will manage. Somehow, we'll manage."

My mother received a cold reception from the other workers at the cotton farm, for they initially suspected she had been recruited by the communists to spy on the workers. As a clerk in a brigade composed of eight men and four tractors, it was my mother's job to schedule work assignments and to regularly report vital farming statistics to the camp supervisor, such as how much land was plowed, how much seed and gas were needed, worker attendance and the like. The supervisor made it very clear to my mother that part of her job was to inflate the figures of her reports.

"If your crew cultivates 25 acres, write down 40," the supervisor commanded. "If we need 10 gallons of gas, tell them 20. They never send us all we request, and central planning sets our production goals so high that it's impossible for us to meet our quota."

"I understand," replied my mother.

My mother also understood that she was being set up for execution by the supervisor. Each farm received regular visits from communist inspectors. When the inspectors discovered that a collective was over estimating supplies, they sought out the guilty party and executed them on the spot. Because my mother was signing the requisitions for supplies, it was her life on the line.

The workers were forced to stay at the collective around the clock, which meant my mother was allowed to return home on an overnight furlough every other Saturday. Mrs. L moved into our mud hut and looked after me, and her warm, loving demeanor and quick laugh made her a perfect substitute for my mother. My mother saved the flour from her rations at the cotton farm and brought it home to feed to me. Miraculously, my health improved, and before long I was back to work with Mrs. L, scouring the countryside for firewood and food.

Our lives became as dreary and predictable as the drizzling rain that fell ceaselessly during Uzbekistan's long winter. My stomach ached and grumbled continually, and each day our spirits dropped as our rations disappeared.

Surprise Visitor

One afternoon as Mrs. L and I were listening to a drizzling rain drumming against the roof, I pulled my threadbare quilt tighter around my neck and stared helplessly at our dwindling supply of firewood. Without warning Mrs. L's thin, slumping body jerked to attention.

"My goodness," she blurted, shaking her head from side to side as if to clear her thoughts. "Did I see what I thought I saw?"

She leaned sideways, swaying like a cobra while squinting at the gaps in the straw door. I tossed off my quilt and ran to the open window. I was amazed to see two stray chickens pecking in the mud a few feet from our hut.

"Mrs. L," I whispered loudly. "Could we capture one?" The woman's jaw dropped, but she didn't reply.

"Please, Mrs. L," I persisted. "Just one. They're so close. Let's trap one before they run off." I hesitated before adding, "Wouldn't mother be surprised?"

"Well ..." Mrs. L. chewed at her thumbnail as she pondered my suggestion. It had been more than a year since the woman had seen a chicken, much less tasted one, and her mouth watered at the prospect of biting into grilled chicken breast. Still, she hesitated for a moment, mulling over the consequences of getting caught. Suddenly, she sprung into action.

"I'll find some seed while you get dressed," Mrs. L blurted, and she smiled and motioned for me to hurry as she gathered up a handful of dirty seeds. In minutes Mrs. L and I were strolling outdoors in the direction of the chickens, casually dropping a trail of seeds that led back inside our hut.

"I could be killed for this if anyone catches us," Mrs. L groaned as we trudged through the mud and drizzling rain.

"Then let's hope no one sees us," I whispered as we hurried through the doorway.

"Let's hope one of these chickens isn't beyond temptation," she countered as we stationed ourselves on either side of the entrance.

Before long one of the chickens bobbed and pecked her way through our doorway, oblivious to our ambush. Mrs. L lunged at the chicken, seizing the startled bird by its throat while I slammed the flimsy straw door behind us. Mrs. L reached into her apron pocket and pulled out a long-bladed knife, awkwardly sawing it across the chicken's scrawny neck.

"I've never done this before," Mrs. L wailed as she awkwardly sawed at the neck of the violently kicking, twisting chicken. With a look of horror and panic, Mrs. L finally succeeded in cutting through the chicken's neck, only to discover she was left holding its head while the chicken ran haphazardly around the hut, blood pumping from its neck.

"Don't just stand there, child," she squealed as she grabbed at the mud-caked hem of her skirt, pulling it above her bony knees. "Help me grab a leg."

With a clumsy, high-stepping movement, Mrs. L rushed at the headless, blood-soaked chicken, dodging first forward, then back, as the erratic bird ricocheted randomly around the hut.

All of this happened so quickly I was frozen with horror. But the more I surveyed this unlikely scene — a bony aristocrat wildly flapping her arms and prancing erratically, perfectly mirroring the flailing antics of a headless, blood-spewing chicken — the more I felt the urge to laugh.

I covered my mouth with my hands, but it was no use. Convulsions of laughter poured out of me as my grim-faced babysitter hunched over the epileptic chicken, smothering its death-defying dance in long fingers that were far more accustomed to playing piano sonatas than butchering barnyard animals.

I continued to laugh even as the headless chicken slowly jerked to a standstill. Laughter poured out of me as I fell weak-kneed to the ground. My laughter was a dam-burst of relief. I laughed because we didn't get caught. I laughed because I'd soon be eating the first good meal I'd had in two years. I laughed because there were so few occasions for laughter amidst all our misery. I laughed because I somehow knew I would choke on hopelessness unless I released my heartache in a laugh.

"When you are finally able to control your mirth, Miss Dabrowska, would you please start a fire?" Mrs. L said with mock sternness as a slow smile crossed her triumphant face. "Let's get this chicken cooked right away!"

I quickly gathered up the last of the wet cotton branches and lit a fire while Mrs. L did her best to pluck the feathers out by hand. Because our kindling was too wet to produce a decent fire, we had to wait patiently for the bird to cook in a pot of water suspended over a flameless, smoldering heat. The aroma of slowly stewing chicken filled the room for hours, tormenting Mrs. L and me with the anticipation of our upcoming feast, as well as the anxiety that the owner would discover his prized chicken in our pot.

"We finally find ourselves a decent meal," Mrs. L lamented as she stirred the thickening broth, "and I can't even savor the aroma for fear we will be discovered. If the wrong person catches a whiff of our dinner, I'll end up in worse shape than this bird!" she said with a comic frown.

I giggled at her joke, but we both knew our offense was a serious one in Uzbekistan. But our fears were dispelled once we began feasting on the tender chicken.

"This is the best chicken I've ever tasted," I exclaimed as I sucked a slender slice of white meat off a bone.

"I couldn't agree more," rejoined Mrs. L, ignoring for the moment that just a few years ago a scrawny, under-cooked chicken like this one wouldn't have been fit fare for her servants.

"Let's save a big piece for Mamma," I giggled.

"Yes, we must," said Mrs. L. "Your mother will be delighted to see that you and I can manage quite well while she and your father are away."

Mrs. L and I spent the rest of the evening eating and laughing contentedly. Our meal turned into a celebration of love and survival, and for the moment our spirits escaped the cold, wet bonds of the Land of the Dead and soared heavenward like tiny, brightly burning embers.

For this one, singular moment, in a tiny mud hut on an endless plain of gray mud in a dreary southern province of Russia called Uzbekistan, I was happy. And I reveled in my moment of happiness, for I knew that more misery — as steady and constant as the cold, endless rain — was patiently waiting for us outside.

8

Escape From the Land of the Dead

M y mother's hand trembled on a cold March day in 1942 as she held my father's dirty, crumpled letter in her hand. She hesitated before opening it, fearing the letter contained unbearable news.

You must come to Kerminech as soon as possible, my father had written in a hastily scribbled note. His division had received orders to be stationed in private homes in the desert outside Kerminech, a small city 500 miles from us near the southern border of Uzbekistan. From there his division would be driven to a port on the Caspian Sea and shipped south to Iran for a brief stopover before departing for Italy, where the Polish army would engage the relentless Germans.

"We must find a way to Kerminech before it's too late," my mother said sternly. "Come with me, Alicia. We have no time to spare!"

With my mother leading the way, we hurried to the train station at Sarasyja. Black clouds of smoke belched from the smoke-

55

stack of the empty train, covering everything and everyone at the station in a thin veil of soot. My mother waited patiently in line to see how much it would cost for the three of us to travel to Kerminech.

"I'm sorry, but I'm not allowed to sell tickets to civilians," the station master explained. "These trains are to be used exclusively for military personnel and equipment."

"We only need three tickets to Kerminech," replied my mother. "My husband is in the Polish army with the seventh division field artillery. He's waiting for us."

"I'm sorry," the man said firmly, "but it's impossible for me to sell tickets to you or any other civilian. The matter is beyond my control." The station master shrugged his shoulders in a gesture of helplessness.

My mother walked slowly away from the ticket window, but I could tell by her expression that she was mulling over all of her options. Although my mother was a tiny woman, her will was as strong as an Olympic champion's, and she seldom took "no" for an answer when she was determined to get her way.

Time for the Silk

"There are two things you can be sure of, Mr. Station Master," she muttered to herself on the way back to our hut. "One, there is a way for us to get on that train and two, I will find it."

Upon returning home, my mother opened her battered suitcase and removed the flawless piece of green silk, running her hand over the smooth finish.

"I've been saving this for a very special occasion," my mother said flatly. "And now, I think, that occasion is upon us."

Tucking the silk cloth under her arm, my mother headed back to the train station to look for the station master's wife, who my mother was certain would covet a gift as rare as silk.

Sure enough, the station master's wife found the shimmering green silk irresistible. She readily agreed to have her husband arrange to transport the three of us to Kerminech. Within days we received instructions to meet the station master and his wife at the coal bin of the troop train. We immediately packed and left our mud hut, the flimsy door open and flapping in the wind.

After the silk was safely transferred to the beaming wife, the station master cautiously introduced us to his brother, who was the train engineer. He glanced around nervously before instructing us to hide in the train's coal bin. We huddled silently inside the sooty chamber as grim-faced KGB agents paced from car to car, searching for unauthorized personnel. There was good reason for the station master and his brother to be nervous, for harboring stowaways was considered treason and, if discovered, stowaways were immediately removed from the train and shot. We listened to the heavy boots of the KGB as they stomped down the aisles of the train cars, covering our mouths with our dresses and breathing shallowly to prevent coughing in the dusty bin.

After the train churned into motion and the lights from the train station were no longer visible, the station master's brother signaled for us to come out of hiding and mingle with the other passengers as if we were the family of an army officer. We settled into an unoccupied corner of one of the cars, and made ourselves as inconspicuous as possible, our movements restricted to infrequent trips to the toilets. Two days later mother, Mrs. L, and I were dusting ourselves off on the platform of the Kerminech train depot, discussing the best way to go about finding a place to stay.

Because there were so many displaced Poles throughout Russia during this time, it didn't take us long to find a tent city populated by a small gathering of Polish refugees. We were invited to share a tent with another family, and we readily accepted.

As it turned out, my mother had made a good decision in leaving her job at the cotton collective. The civilians in Kerminech received modest rations, which meant we weren't in immediate danger of starving to death. But even with the improved rations, we were still constantly hungry, and we spent our days searching for extra food, just as we had done in Uzbekistan. One day we were fortunate to capture a turtle, and that evening we savored our delicacy, and we laughed into the night recalling the bout Mrs. L had with the chicken a few weeks earlier.

Frequently the Polish soldiers would share their provisions with us, enjoying the conversations about the days before the war and seeking information about lost loved ones. From these conversations my mother determined that my father's division was probably still camped in desert homes several miles outside the city. Since there were not plans for his division to move out, my mother decided to stay in Kerminech and wait.

Several months passed by, and we still had not heard from my father. It was obvious our wait-and-see strategy wasn't going to lead to a reunion with my father anytime soon. At the end of May the tent-dwellers at Kerminech were transported to Guzary, a dreary, impoverished village located in the southern-most part of Uzbekistan. Once again we were being moved around like pawns on a giant political chessboard. Guzary was a step backward for us. Our rations were cut back to a daily allotment of rice and water.

The only good thing that came from the relocation to Guzary was an unlikely blessing for Mrs. L. We came to find out that one of Mrs. L's sons had spent several years traveling from one refugee camp to another looking for his mother. Miraculously, he found her in Guzary, and they spent several days in a blissful, tearful reunion before departing for his home back in Poland.

My mother and I rejoiced in Mrs. L's new-found happiness, for her age and her lack of useful skills made her especially vulnerable to the inevitable hardships that awaited us. We were delighted to be a part of her reunion with her son, but, in the same breath, we were saddened, for we had grown to love this remarkably cheerful, selfless woman whose bright flame of hope had illuminated our black misery during our time together.

The consensus among the thousands of Polish refugees was that the Russians didn't know what to do with us, especially the women and children who couldn't help them in their battle with the Germans. We decided that the Russians' plan was to systematically kill us off by cutting our rations and moving us from one desolate desert town to another. Each time the Russians ordered us to move, the Polish population was thinned by starvation, dysentery, cholera, and despair.

Our destiny was in the hands of the ruthless Russians unless we did something drastic soon. It became more and more obvious to my mother that we had to make some drastic decisions or we would end up dead or, even worse, prisoners inside communist Russia for the rest of our lives. We had to find some way to escape before the Iron Curtain came down with a deafening crash.

I was only nine years old at the time, but I sensed my mother's increasing frustration.

"Tell me what I can do to help you, Mamma," I offered.

"I don't know ... I don't know what to do," she stammered as she pulled me closer.

"Do you think we're going to die?" I asked quietly. There was a long silence while my mother carefully shaped her reply. This was no time to coddle a child with a naive answer. This moment wasn't about soothing the fears of a little girl who just woke up from a bad dream. This was about survival, and we both knew it.

"I don't believe that we can survive here alone," my mother said calmly. "We must get away from here. We must."

"We have to be strong, Mamma," I said. "God will take care of us."

"Yes, of course you're right, darling."

After witnessing and experiencing two years of unspeakable horrors, the relationship between my mother and me was more like that of two dear friends who were bound by shared personal tragedies than mother and daughter. My innocence had long been destroyed, as if it were a porcelain doll ground to dust under the black iron wheels of a locomotive.

"I can be strong like you and Father," I insisted. "I know I can. Do you think we should leave Guzary now?"

"Yes, we must escape right away," my mother sighed with sad resignation. "But the two of us wouldn't last long on foot. Our only chance for escape is to join a group that provides rations and transportation. There is strength in numbers."

My mother rose to her feet to pace the floor while she built up the courage to tell me of a plan that she had been mulling over for several days.

The Orphanage at Guzary

"Alicia," she said after several minutes of deep thought. "I've thought of a plan that could save us."

She stopped her pacing and looked lovingly at me, and I remember feeling sad that my mother had been placed in a situation where she couldn't wrap her arms around her only child and brush the ugly world away in the same way that she would gently smooth my hair from my face with her hand.

"I think our best chance for survival," my mother said as

she bit down hard on her bottom lip, "is for me to join the Polish army and for you to stay in a children's home. It's our best chance to travel in a group and escape from Russia before the communists close the borders.

"Right now," she continued, "Polish refugees are a nuisance to the Russians. But it won't be long before the communists organize us into slave-labor camps to help with their war effort. When that happens, we'll never be allowed to leave this country alive. That's why we must act now."

My mother hung her head for a moment before raising her face to look directly into my eyes. I understood immediately the full, awful impact of my mother's proposal. I'd be on my own for weeks, perhaps months, at a time. After all, my father had joined the army, and it had been months since we'd last seen him.

I wanted to be brave, but I looked into my lap to avoid my mother's eyes. Wasn't there some other way that we could escape and still be together?

"I know, dear," my mother cooed, stroking my down-turned face. "I'll miss you, too. But we have so much to look forward to. Once the three of us are safely out of Russia, we will build a new life together."

My mother sat on the floor and patted her lap for me to join her. I wrapped my arms around her and nestled into her lap as she rocked slowly back and forth, as we took turns whispering prayers into the silent night.

The next day my mother applied for induction and was issued an immediate reporting date. A Polish woman whose two children were living at the orphanage in Guzary advised my mother to let me approach the orphanage alone to increase my chances of being accepted as a ward.

I can still remember the morning that my mother was scheduled to report to duty. We walked hand in hand together to the children's home before stopping outside the entrance gate.

"I'm sorry I can't go in with you, darling," my mother said somberly. "If the people in the orphanage see that you have a mamma, they may not let you stay."

"It's all right, Mamma," I replied. "I'm not afraid."

"You are a brave little girl, Alicia, and I love you with all my heart."

"I love you, too," I replied with a trembling lip.

"Darling, I don't know when I'll be able to come visit you." my mother said solemnly. "Soon, I pray." My mother paused to dab at a tear forming in the corner of her eye.

"When you come back," I said, "we'll get out of Russia. We'll be together, Mamma, and we won't die. I just know it!"

I nuzzled my mother's soft neck and touched her thick, dark hair. "We have to be strong, Mamma, like when Daddy had to leave to join the army."

I could see the teardrops sparkling on my mother's long eyelashes as she moved her face to kiss my forehead. She hugged me long and hard before rising from her knees and urging me toward the front gate.

"I love you," I cried as I half turned and blew a kiss in my mother's direction.

"I love you, too, Alicia. Be brave. Be strong." She smiled and waved stiffly as I turned and entered through the rusted iron gates.

I've thought about this episode a thousand times over the years, and it never fails to bring a lump to my throat. Can you imagine facing a decision like the one my mother faced, and then having the courage to usher your nine-year-old child to the front door of an orphanage, never knowing when, or if, you would ever see her again?

The memory still breaks my heart, even though it's been over half a century since I stood in front of an orphanage in a poor village in a barren land in a Godless country caught in the angry fist of a world drunk on innocent blood.

Imagine for a moment that you were in my mother's shoes ... and then imagine escorting your nine-year-old child to the front gates of a dilapidated orphanage inside communist Russia. And then answer this question: If this episode happened to you, would you be absolutely, completely passionate about spreading the message of freedom throughout the world?

By answering this question, perhaps you have a better understanding of my passion for freedom and for my mission in life namely, to do whatever it takes to make sure that there will never again be an occasion when a mother is so desperate to be free that she is forced to say good-bye to her daughter at the gates of an orphanage.

Never again, I say. NEVER AGAIN!

After I passed through the gates of the orphanage, I was surprised to discover a long line of children waiting at the side entrance. I noticed immediately that I was the smallest child in the group. The other children were easily a foot taller than I!

"They'll never take you shorty," a freckle-faced boy teased. "You have to be at least 12 years old to get in this place."

I was suddenly frozen with fear. What if the orphanage wouldn't take me and my mother was already gone? Where would I go? Who would take care of me? *They must take me,* I thought to myself. *They must!*

I threw my shoulders back and walked toward the admissions officer, standing on tiptoe as he questioned me. The man looked me over from head to foot. Even though I was almost nine years old, I was so small and undernourished that I could have passed for six. Perhaps the admissions officer felt sorry for me. Or perhaps he was impressed with a tiny, half-starved girl who was bold enough to stand on her tiptoes and try to bluff her way into the orphanage. Whatever the reason, I was admitted to the facility with a wink and a smile.

If my mother were aware of the living conditions in the orphanage, I'm certain she would have devised a different plan for our escape from Russia. In many ways the conditions of the Mala Jeluga labor camp were better than the orphanage's. The place was an open breeding ground for disease. We slept side by side on filthy bare floors, inches away from coughing, wheezing children sick or dying from cholera and tuberculosis. Dozens of children died each week from Malaria alone, and virtually every child was sick with advanced dysentery. The open-air latrines were stained with blood, and I will forever remember the hideous sight of intestines bulging from the rectums of dying children, some of whom had become my friends.

We received a small bowl of rice three times a day and one teaspoon of sugar — a special treat that I stored in a matchbox. The only water available to us came from a foul-smelling, open well, and the bitter taste of the dark-gray liquid made us wretch violently. One day some of the older boys were poking wooden poles into the well when they struck a large, mysterious object floating just beneath the surface. The boys pulled the object to the surface and discovered it was a fully dressed, decomposing body of a teenage girl! This was our drinking water! It's a miracle that we all didn't die from cholera.

My weakened immune system finally broke down completely, and one morning I awoke bathed in perspiration, too weak to move, every joint in my body racked with pain. I moved in and out of delirium, one minute conscious, miserable, crying ... the next moment lost in a swirling dream world that flashed back and forth from my home in Poland to surreal replaying of the horrors I had witnessed over the last two years.

Miraculously, my mother happened to be visiting me on an overnight furlough. She immediately removed my ragged, filthy clothing and began rubbing my limp, feverish body with cold water. After the cold water bath broke my fever, my mother wrapped me in blankets and gave me fresh water to drink, rocking me in her arms as I mumbled incoherently.

"Dear Heavenly Father," my mother prayed out loud as the tears flowed down her cheeks, "please let my innocent Alicia live."

The next morning I awoke, thirsty and disoriented. I thought I was still dreaming when I looked up to see my mother lightly brushing my forehead and holding my hand. I cried and hugged her endlessly while she fed me small bites from her army rations and encouraged me to take long drinks of cool, fresh water from her canteen. By the time my mother had to leave, I had regained much of my strength.

"Remember, Alicia," she said earnestly. "You have to be strong no matter how difficult life may seem. The three of us are fighting for our lives, and with God's help, we will survive. Never, never give up, my darling!"

While my mother and I battled illness and hunger, my father was being rotated from home to home in Uzbekistan. On August 26, 1942, he finally received his orders to return to Kerminech. He had no way of knowing if we had received his letter, much less managed to travel to Kerminech, but he spent his four-day layover in Kerminech searching for us, unaware that we were already on our way to the port city of Krasnovodsk, Turkmenistan. As my father boarded the train for Krasnovodsk with the other soldiers, he bowed his head for a moment, praying that he would somehow find us among the mass of Polish refugees crowded into the busy port city.

Last Ship from Russia

We'll never know what influenced Stalin's strategies as he moved his pieces on the chessboard of international politics, but this much we do know: Once the Iron Curtain came down completely, Polish citizens trapped in Russia had a choice. They could choose to become Russian citizens, or they could choose to go to jail. Either way, they would never leave Russia alive.

But just before closing off the borders permanently, Stalin made two decisions that would save our lives. First of all, he ordered 100,000 Polish troops to Italy to fight the advancing German army. My father's division was among the reassigned troops.

Second of all, for the time being, Stalin was permitting certain groups other than troops — such as orphans — to leave the country. Most likely it was a political ploy to court international favor. Whatever the reason, the orphanage in Guzary received orders to accompany the caravan of trucks carrying Polish soldiers to Krasnovodsk. My mother and I were part of that caravan.

As soon as the Polish soldiers arrived in Krasnovodsk, they were transported to the docks, where they were herded onto freighters heading to Iran. My father delayed his boarding as long as he could, trying his best to locate us among the crowds of soldiers and civilians. As he sprinted up the gangplank of the freighter *Zhdanov*, my father understood that this was his last chance to escape the iron fist of Stalinism, and he prayed that somehow, someway, his wife and daughter had received his letter and managed to escape from the jaws of the Russian bear before they snapped shut. After a 26-hour voyage on the Caspian Sea, my father disembarked at Pahlevi, a busy seaport in northern Iran.

"Thank you, Father, for delivering me from slavery and death," my father prayed as he fell to his knees in Pahlevi, crumbling a clod of dirt in his hand, relishing the warmth and texture of free soil. "Please guard my family well and bring them to safety and freedom."

Four days after my father's departure from Russia aboard the

Zhdanov, my mother and I arrived in Krasnovodsk, unaware that we had missed a reunion with my father by only a few days. Coincidentally, my mother's division and the children from the orphanage were assigned to board the *Zhdanov*, the same freighter my father sailed days earlier.

I learned later that this was the last time that the *Zhdanov* would be used to transport civilians out of Russia. In fact, it was the last time that any group of civilians was allowed to leave Russia, period. After the *Zhdanov* pulled away from the dock in Krasnovodsk, the Iron Curtain came down with a deafening thud, and would remain down for more than 50 years.

I clutched what was left of my tattered quilt under my chin as I searched the crowded dock for my mother. I spotted a group of Polish soldiers and studied them intently, hoping to spot my mother. Out of the corner of my eye I caught sight of four female soldiers running toward the dock. I immediately recognized one of them — a wisp of a woman with long, dark hair.

"Mother! Mother! Over here!" I shouted as I waived my arms and jumped wildly up and down. She turned and pointed an arm in my direction, and then pointed at the ship, nodding her head up and down to confirm that we were both boarding the *Zhdanov*.

Although my mother and I were traveling on the same ship, we had little opportunity to see each other. The soldiers were sequestered below, while the children were packed so tightly onto the top deck that we were forced to stand for most of the day-and-night voyage.

Misery Boards the Zhdanov

Even so, all of the children cheered for their new-found freedom and waived wildly as we floated from the dock, anticipating that our new destination could only be an improvement over the orphanage. It didn't take us long to realize, however, that although we were escaping from the long arm of communism, we couldn't escape from our misery just yet. Misery had boarded the *Zhdanov*, too.

Minutes into the voyage we were told that there was no food available for the children, which meant that by the time we docked in Iran, we wouldn't have eaten for several days. Most of us were deathly ill with dysentery, and many of the children succumbed to sea sickness, which meant within a few hours of departure the deck was slippery with vomit, urine, and bloody feces.

"We're in hell," wailed an ashen-faced teenage girl as she desperately clawed at the rail to keep her balance. I saw her hand go slack and watched in horror as the frail body slipped to the floor.

"Get up!" I screamed reaching for her hand. "You must get up!"

But there was no response. She was dead. The children watched numbly as two of the strongest boys lifted the lifeless body over the rail and tossed it into the sea.

I covered my eyes and turned my back at the horror of the scene, but my mind immediately flashed back to vivid memories of dead Poles being tossed from Russian cattle cars into deep snowdrifts. Would these living nightmares ever end?

I was still only nine years old, and nine-year-old girls are supposed to be brushing their dolls' hair or licking cookie batter from a wooden spoon or skipping rope on the school playground. Nine-year-old girls weren't supposed to be standing ankle deep in human waste, watching innocent children die from starvation and disease. I resolved to stay alive and remain free, no matter what it took, so that I could witness to the world the horrors I had seen and to expose communism for what it was — a slogan-spouting gang of brutal sadists.

On the third day, the *Zhdanov* docked at Pahlevi, Iran. I reunited with my mother at the top of the gangplank, and we clutched each other as we hobbled down the ramp on unsteady legs. We spent the afternoon walking around the seaport's open market, breathing in the hot air heavy with the smells of cooking fish and fresh manure. Compared to the stench of the ship, the air was perfumed. We watched, fascinated, as dark-skinned vendors clothed in flowing white robes hawked their wares.

"Are we free now, Mamma?" I asked cautiously, unsure of the reply.

"Yes, my darling," came my mother's reply. "We're free now!"

"Does that mean we won't be hungry anymore?" I asked. My mother dropped to her knees and hugged me before delivering her reply.

"What it means," she laughed, tousling my hair, "is that no one can stop us from buying a special treat from that man over there," she said, pointing in the direction of an ice cream vendor. "Come on," my mother shouted as she playfully grabbed my wrist. "Let's get some before it melts!"

We sat under a spreading tree and savored the slowly melting ice cream. I looked in the face of every man in uniform, hoping to see my father. We knew from my father's letter that his division was being transferred to Pahlevi, but mother hadn't received a letter from him in months, so she didn't know if he was in the port city by now or not.

My mother and I longed for a reunion with my father, and we savored the thought of reuniting with my father while we savored our new-found freedom and our melting ice cream. We talked and giggled and hugged as we took in the sights and sounds of this strange, brown land thousands of miles from my familiar green homeland.

Little did we know at the time that it would be six long years before we saw my father again.

9

Lost In Iran

T he day after our ship docked in Iran, the children from the orphanage were assigned temporary quarters in the capital city of Tehran, 150 miles to the south. My mother's military unit also received its orders for reassignment. The Polish soldiers would escort the orphans to Tehran before being transported to Israel, where they would protect the Allied interests in the Middle East.

This meant, of course, that my mother and I would be separated for many months. But we reasoned that this was still my best option for survival, for at least I would receive food and shelter, and she would know where to find me when the war ended.

The trip to Tehran moved at a snail's pace as the trucks rocked and groaned over the unpaved desert roads, and I could feel myself getting hotter and hotter with each mile. At first I thought I was suffering from car sickness. Or possibly the suffocating desert heat. But soon my body began to ache and my head began to throb. By the time the caravan stopped for the night, I was suffering from a severe bout of malaria — one minute shivering from the chills, the next minute drenched by a soaking fever.

My mother briefly left her unit to check on me, and one glance at my flushed face told her immediately that I was suffering a recurring attack of malaria.

"Drink this, dear," my mother said as she held a tin cup of cool water to my lips. She cradled me in her arms and bathed me with cool water to lower my body temperature.

"I have to return to my unit," my mother said apologetically. "But I'll see you first thing in the morning. Be strong, Alicia. Be strong."

I could tell my mother didn't want to leave me in my condition, but she knew if she defied her orders to report to her unit, she could be discharged on the spot. We both needed the daily army rations and the security of a military escort to survive in this unforgiving land.

I spent a restless night, moving in and out of delirium, as my bout with malaria worsened. When I awoke, I ached all over, as if I had contracted a violent case of the flu. The slightest movement sent searing shocks of pain down my arms and legs. To make matters worse, I couldn't open my eyes — they were painfully swollen and sealed shut with a crusty, dried mucus.

"Mamma!" I screamed between sobs. But there was no answer.

Several days later I awoke to hear the soothing voice of a kind Iranian doctor as he gently cleansed my swollen eyes.

"You are in a hospital in Tehran," the doctor said in heavily accented Russian. "The director of the orphanage brought you here a few days ago," he continued. "You're a very sick little girl, but we're giving you medicine for your malaria and your eye infection, and you'll be all well again soon."

The doctor smiled warmly at me and squeezed my tiny wrist in his long, brown fingers. He made me feel completely safe. Months later I was able to piece together the events that led me to this kindly doctor.

Separated In Iran

The day I came down with my attack of malaria, my mother was ordered to leave me and return to her unit for the night. She assured me she would return at the break of dawn to check on me. But the trucks carrying the orphans left hours ahead of schedule, long before sunrise. Because my condition continued to deteriorate during the night, the director of the orphanage arranged to have me dropped off at the nearest hospital in Tehran. My mother's division stopped long enough in Tehran to gas up and take on fresh water before continuing south on their road to Israel, more than 1,000 miles to the west.

I soon realized that my mother and I had been separated. I was completely alone, and I shuddered at the thought that neither of my parents knew where to find me. Here I was, a malnourished nine-year-old, deathly ill with malaria and fighting a serious eye infection, a little blond-haired, fair-skinned girl lost in a country of dark-skinned natives whose language and culture were completely foreign to me.

At least I have food and a place to stay, I thought to myself. *And I have a kind, smiling doctor to look after me. God will see that Mother finds me. I just know it. I must be strong.*

I looked forward to my doctor's morning visits, and I got in the habit of listening for his brisk, light footsteps outside my door. But one day the doctor didn't pay his usual visit. In fact, the smiling doctor didn't visit any of his patients. One of the nurses said he was called away for a few days on a medical emergency. I was alone again. Completely, utterly alone. I prayed that my smiling doctor would return to me again soon.

Released from the Hospital

"Nurse, release this young lady immediately!" barked a sober-faced doctor. I couldn't believe what I was hearing. *Who is this man? Where is my kind doctor? Where will I go? Who will take care of me?*

I begged to talk to my doctor — the gentle, smiling man who had taken good care of me.

"He won't be back for several more days," came the gruff reply. "You've been here a month. It's time to make room for someone who is really sick. You'll be fine."

Within minutes a nurse stripped off my hospital gown, rolled it up with my bedding, and headed out the door, leaving me sitting naked on a wood bench. The nurse reappeared in the doorway carrying a small bundle that contained everything I owned — one pair of panties and a torn, gray slip, the outfit I was wearing when I was admitted to the hospital a month earlier.

I walked barefooted out of the hospital and onto the crowded street, rubbing my swollen eyes and squinting to avoid the painfully bright sunlight. I must have been a sight in this modest, Moslem country — a pale, blond-haired, blue-eyed child in her underwear struggling to move against a swelling tide of darkskinned adults clothed in long, flowing white gowns. Pedestrians stopped and stared, pointing and laughing at such an unlikely sight. A few passers-by reached out to touch my hair as they swept past me like white-caps on a rough brown sea.

In the distance I could see scores of billowing tents like the ones that dotted the dock in Pahlevi, and I headed in their direction, figuring it was a marketplace. As I entered the marketplace, I collapsed on a small wooden crate next to a vegetable stand. I held my aching head in my hands, pulled my quilt up to cover my face, and burst into tears.

God, what am I to do next, I sobbed to myself. *Am I going to starve to death? Please, God, don't let me die now that I'm finally free.*

I'd survived without food before, but at least I'd always had someone to love and care for me. But now I was alone. Completely, terrifyingly alone.

If I give up now, I said to myself, *I'll never see my parents again. There must be something I can do.* I eyed the plump, fresh sugar beets in the open bin next to me. For a moment I was tempted to grab one and run, but I decided that stealing was not the answer to my problem.

I'll move on, I said to myself. *God is with me. Nothing is impossible!*

I spent the afternoon exploring the streets of Tehran. By evening I was starved and exhausted. My feet were cut and bruised, my legs numb from hours of walking. I sat down and rested against a wall, trying to decide where I would spend the night.

God, I prayed aloud, *if you're going to take me, take me now. I'm too tired to go on and I'm hopelessly lost ...*

My desperate prayer was interrupted by familiar voices coming from a nearby tent. Were they speaking Polish? Yes, yes, it was Polish! I jumped up and ran toward the voices, dragging my quilt in the dust behind me. I couldn't believe what I saw. I stopped and dabbed at my eyes and opened them painfully wide. It was a group of light-skinned people. My God, they were Polish refugees!

"I'm Polish, too! I'm Polish, too!" I shouted as I ran crying toward the group, throwing my arms around the legs of the nearest person.

"What are you doing here? Can you help me?" I pleaded.

The small band of Polish refugees fed me crusts of bread and fresh water. I gobbled down the bread while they patiently told me their plans. I had somehow stumbled across a makeshift Polish refugee center. They were waiting for a truck to transport them south to a port city on the Persian Gulf, where they would board a cargo ship sailing out of the Persian Gulf, through the Arabian Sea to Bombay, India, before veering southwest across the Indian Ocean to a permanent refugee camp in Tanzania, a British colony on the east coast of Africa. With stopovers, the 5,000-mile trip would take more than two months.

"May I go, too?" I asked anxiously. "I've lost my mother and father, and I have no place to go."

"Of course you can go," an old man chuckled. "We'll sign you up for the trip tomorrow. And I'll personally take you to the infirmary tomorrow, where they can treat your swollen eyes."

It took two weeks for the truck to arrive to drive us 600 or so miles across the heartland of Iran to the seaport on the Persian Gulf. I stayed close to the group, leaving only occasionally to wait in line for treatment at the eye clinic. A sympathetic doctor gave me an extra tube of ointment to use during the long voyage to Africa.

I hesitated at the bottom of the cargo ship's boarding ramp as memories of the nightmare voyage aboard the *Zhdanov* flashed across my memory. For a terrifying moment I imagined the ship was a gigantic sea monster hugging the shoreline and that the boarding plank was its tongue.

"Don't be afraid, little one," said a kindly old man as he coaxed me forward. "Here, take my arm. I need you to help me aboard."

I cautiously guided the man toward the gaping mouth of the cargo hold, and together, hand-in-hand, we entered the mouth of the beast.

I spent most of the voyage rocking silently in my fishnet hammock, praying for a cool breeze in the stifling tropical heat as the unnamed cargo ship sliced a diagonal course across the equator. As much as I dreaded the hot, humid days, I hated the nights even more, for in the darkness I could hear the rats as they scurried across the steel-plate deck and gnawed hungrily on the thick nautical ropes.

I was further tormented by the thoughts of the large, spindly legged spiders that roamed the ships at night. I would wake up screaming every time I felt a tickle on my legs or arms, terrified it was a nest of hungry spiders coming to devour me.

The adults looked after me as best they could, saving scraps from their rations for me to eat, but food didn't interest me much by this time. What I needed most was food for the soul — love. I longed for my mother's light hands smoothing my hair, my father's strong arms hugging my waist.

Will Mommy and Daddy find me in Africa? I wondered silently as the ship swayed toward its destination.

Dear, God, please let them find me! Please! I cried into the heavy, damp air. The only reply was the dull, predictable thud of the waves slapping against the hull.

10
The Green Hills of Africa

A frica — green, green Africa.

Nothing could have prepared me for what I was about to see when our ship sailed into Mombasa, Kenya, a busy industrial port near the northern border of Tanganyika, known today as Tanzania. For three years I had lived in barren wastelands — first in frozen Siberia, then in rock-littered Uzbekistan, and finally in the endless deserts of Iran.

Africa was the other side of the world in every way, and I was instantly fascinated by this strange, exotic continent. I stood leaning against the ship's railing, studying the tall, thin, black-skinned village women draped from head to toe in bright scarves and bold-striped blankets.

I watched the women for hours as they balanced straw baskets of ripe fruit on their heads while carrying fat, sleeping babies strapped to their backs. Their long, slender arms were stacked with silver bracelets, and layers of shiny hoops circled their necks. The women laughed and sang as they moved gracefully across the docks, their red and green and yellow scarves fluttering in the breeze, their metal bracelets accompanying their voices like wind chimes. For a little girl who had seen nothing but sick-gray mud in Uzbekistan and dead-brown sand in Iran, Africa was a magical, color-drenched land of enchantment.

"No time to daydream," said a gruff voice behind me, breaking my reverie. "Move quickly! The trucks are waiting for us!"

We were loaded onto large, fat-wheeled trucks that crawled and twisted their way though thick green forests on the way to Tengeru, an abandoned village deep inside the country near Lake Tanganyika. The once-vibrant village was situated in a small clearing near the base of majestic, snow-capped Mt. Kilimanjaro, the highest mountain in Africa. As we pulled into the clearing, we expected to see a farming village, complete with a cluster of shops and homes that required some fixing up.

But we were months too late, for the village had already been reclaimed by the relentless jungle. All that remained of the village were high mounds draped with blankets of leaves and tangled vines. Machete-wielding drivers hacked at the strangling foliage to reveal several round, clay huts with cone-shaped roofs made of banana leaves and straw. These huts were called *tukulas*, and each one had a wood door, two windows, and a dirt floor.

The refugees immediately went to work, hacking away at the vines and scattering poison in and around the *tukulas* to kill the snakes and rodents. The refugees worked long days, their clothes soaked through with sweat, their arms and legs a red grid of slashes from the thorny vines. Day by day a small village began to emerge out of the wilderness as the workers spent hours purging the huts of thorny brush littered with the remains of dead reptiles and rodents. Mt. Kilimanjaro stood in the distance, patiently watching as yet another tribe of humans fought to claim a corner of the jungle for themselves.

I wasn't asked to help with the clean-up, and I welcomed the rest, for although my eyes had cleared up, I was still suffering from symptoms of malaria — my head ached continually, and I was always tired and weak. I sat on a grassy spot under a shade tree, content to watch as a village of sturdy brown buildings slowly emerged from the tentacles of the green jungle.

One of the buildings was shaped like the rest of the *tukulas*, but it was narrow and much longer than the others. I learned that this was my new home, the Tengeru orphanage, funded mostly

by donations from Polish soldiers. The lodging was an improvement over our mud hut in Uzbekistan, but not by much. A mud
hut, I discovered, is pretty much a mud hut, no matter where you
are, but at least in Africa, I wasn't chilled to the bone every minute
of the day.

Although I wasn't in danger of starving in my new "home,"
our meals were as predictable as the hot, humid weather — a
bowl of watery oatmeal for breakfast, lunch, and dinner. We attended classes at a school a little over a mile from the village,
which occupied most of our days, and, as you may well guess, school
supplies were scarce to non-existent. The school stationery was
toilet paper, which we used in composing our daily letters to the
soldiers who were supporting us.

I wrote an endless stream of letters to my mother and father
in care of the Polish army. In effect, my letters were a diary of my
longing and my loneliness, a catharsis to unburden my pain:

"Mother, I have no clothes to wear, just my underwear."

"Father, I have no money, and nothing to trade."

"Mamma, sometimes the other children give me mango peals
to suck on."

"Daddy, I feel ashamed. I stole a lemon from a native woman.
I need money to pay her for it."

*"Mother, I know that I am not an orphan. Please come for me
soon."*

Later I discovered that my father only received one of my letters, which at least meant he knew where I was and that I was
safe. One day I was on my way outside to play ball with the other
children when I noticed a smudged, gray envelope resting face
down on my straw mat.

Please let it be a letter from Mamma, I prayed silently as I
reached for the envelope, turning it over to reveal the address.

To: Alicia Dabrowski.

From: Joseph Dabrowski.

"Father!" I shouted as I clutched the envelope to my heart.
"Papa has found me!" I tore open the envelope and unfolded the
letter, pleasantly startled as several pieces of paper money floated
to the floor at my feet.

"Oh, my God," I screamed. "It's money! My daddy sent me

money! Thank you, dear God, for helping my parents find me. I knew I wasn't an orphan. I knew it!"

That night, curled up on my pallet, I barely heard the dull thud of distant jungle drums. I tossed and turned, one moment dreaming of the reunion with my parents, the next moment dreaming of the food and clothes I would buy at the market tomorrow. I finally fell asleep with my father's letter pressed against my breast, my tiny hand still clutching the neatly folded paper money. I later used the money to buy a dress, shoes, socks, and some fruit, my first new possessions in years!

When the director of the orphanage asked me if I wanted to live with a childless family in the settlement, I thought it was the answer to my prayers. It wasn't until I moved in with the couple that I discovered their true motive — they wanted a live-in servant.

The Wilkowskis approached the director of the orphanage, offering to care for a strong young boy in their home. For some unknown reason, the director asked if I would like to stay in the orphanage or live with a middle-aged Polish couple. Desperate for affection and approval, I agreed to move in with them. When I arrived at their hut, I expected a friendly greeting from a warm, loving couple like my parents. Instead, all I got was a cold, blank stare from Mrs. Wilkowski.

"A girl?" the sour-faced woman groaned. "And a tiny, little girl at that. What shall we do?" she whined in the direction of her frowning husband.

"Well," her husband growled, stroking his beard, "we'll have to make the best of it, for the time being, at least."

Mrs. Wilkowski lost no time spelling out my daily chores and telling me how I was to go about doing them. Every day I helped gather and prepare the food, hauled buckets of fresh water from a nearby stream, washed clothes, swept the hard dirt floor, and planted and tended a vegetable garden.

Despite my best efforts, however, the Wilkowskis never seemed satisfied with my work. I was too slow or too fast. Too careless or too thorough. Too dependent or too independent. In short, I was the scapegoat for the couple's unhappiness. To complicate matters, I had developed such an aversion to slavery during the last few horrific years that I bitterly resented my role as a servant. I was more than willing to work. But I would never, ever be willing to serve. Even though I was only a child, barely nine years old, I made a conscious decision to never surrender my freedom. Not for communism. Not for money. And certainly not for sour, mean-spirited people like the Wilkowskis!

Another Bout with Malaria

One afternoon I collapsed at the doorstep after spending the afternoon clearing brush from the side of the *tukula*. Mrs. Wilkowski stood over me and shook her head disapprovingly.

"Now who'll finish the job?" she asked sternly. Clutching Mrs. Wilkowski's arm for support, I staggered to my feet. My cheeks were flushed with fever, yet I was shivering from a deep chill. I was entering the first stages of another bout with malaria.

I was assigned a cot in our village hospital, diagnosed with malaria and an attack of the mumps! In spite of the pain and waves of nausea, I was relieved to be away from the Wilkowskis. I spent much of my time in isolation, resting to regain my strength and dreaming of a reunion with my parents. I hated the idea of returning to the domineering couple, but I knew the orphanage was overcrowded and under-funded, which meant I must return to the Wilkowskis when my health improved. I was in no hurry to leave the hospital.

"Alicia, there's a woman outside who wants to see you," the nurse said cheerfully. "I told her that she wasn't allowed to come inside," the nurse continued, "but you can see her through your window."

I stiffened at the announcement, knowing that the visitor was Mrs. Wilkowski wanting to know when I could get back to work. I ran my hand over my forehead and swollen jaws, reconfirming that I was too sick to be released just yet.

"You won't make me leave just yet, will you?" I asked the nurse with an exaggerated pout.

"Of course not, silly goose," the nurse replied cheerfully. "You'll stay right here until you're well. I'll be back with your medicine in a moment, dear. And don't forget about your visitor," she said with a smile as she turned and headed out the door.

Confident that I was in no danger of being released from the hospital, I pulled myself off the infirmary cot and shuffled to the window, expecting to see the grim-faced Mrs. Wilkowski asking when I would be returning. I figured a quick wave and a long face would discourage her from visiting again anytime soon.

I leaned against the open window, shading my eyes with my hand and squinting into the bright sunlight. My eyes gradually focused on my visitor, a petite, beautiful woman with dark, wavy hair.

"Mamma!"

11

A New Beginning

It had taken six months from the time of our separation in Iran for my mother to find out where I was and to make travel arrangements to join me. As a result, she shadowed me everywhere her first two weeks in Tengeru, terrified that we might somehow become separated again.

The separation had been hard on both of us, for we longed for each other's company. But by necessity, I had become increasingly independent during our time apart, and it didn't take long for me to rebel against my mother's over-protectiveness.

"Look at me, Mother ... see how high I can climb!" I shouted from the top of a sturdy tree. I could hear my mother pleading with me to come down, but that only encouraged me to climb even higher. For several months after our reunion, I looked for any and all occasions to defy my mother's authority over me. I was determined to assert my independence — my wildness, if you will — in a land that encouraged and nurtured my unbridled freedom.

"Watch this, Mother!" I cried as I shimmied to the end of a sturdy limb that extended over a steep ravine. More than 200 feet below, a rushing, muddy river snaked its way across the green landscape like a jagged gray scar. As my mother watched help-lessly, I slid my body off the limb and grabbed it with both hands, swinging back and forth like a trapeze artist.

I could see my mother cover her mouth in alarm as I rocked back and forth, and I smiled broadly at her, enjoying my new-found power, delighting in the fact that I could manipulate her emotions with my reckless behavior.

Rebelling Against My Mother

I had been on my own for almost a year now, and during the previous six months, I'd been living like a feral child on the wild continent of Africa. Because I was small, I looked much younger than my age, but make no mistake about it, I was by no means an innocent, little 10-year-old girl. My innocence had been crushed under the cold, steel wheels of a boxcar three years earlier.

As a result, I was determined to re-draw the boundaries of our relationship. My mother was just as determined to assert her authority over me, and we spent the next few months in a constant stand-off between two strong-willed people.

We were acting out a classic mother-daughter battle of wills that normally takes place during the daughter's turbulent teen-age years. Given my horrific experiences, I was 10 going on 40, and as I reflect on this brief period of rebellion against my mother, I realize that there was no better place in the world to work through our private battle of wills than the wild, untamed continent of Africa.

Every week I wrote my father letters filled with accounts of our adventures in Africa. I wrote about the mundane, everyday challenges of living in a far-away tropical land, like our daily battle with the armies of ants that threatened to overrun our lives. I wrote about how we had to protect our possessions against voracious termites that could reduce a pair of sandals to dust within a few days. I wrote about the occasions we had to stand on the rooftops, wildly waiving blankets and brooms, to prevent dark clouds of locusts from devouring the crops on the neighboring farms. I wrote about the tall, proud Masai tribesmen who would sometimes entertain themselves by menacing us with their spears. And I wrote about our constant vigilance against poisonous snakes and how we had to check our bedding and walls before lying down to sleep at night.

I wrote about grand adventures, too, like our truck ride to the Serengeti Plains, where we explored the Ngorongoro Crater, and I wrote of our weekend trips to Mt. Kilimanjaro and our safaris into the wilderness, where we saw herds of rhinos, elephants, gazelles, and hundreds of other animals in the world's greatest natural habitat.

The time passed quickly in Africa. Weeks melted into months and months into years. Amazingly, it had been six years since I had last seen my father. I was a little nine-year-old girl, lying sick in bed clutching my tattered feather quilt, when I watched helplessly as my father disappeared through the doorway of our mud hut in the Land of the Dead to join the Polish army. By the time my mother and I were packing to leave Africa in 1948, I had grown into a self-reliant 15-year-old.

It was 1943 when I first arrived in Tengeru, and the war was still raging across Europe and Asia. The postmarks on my father's letters chronicled his travels during the war — from Russia to the Middle East to Italy. In 1945 Germany surrendered and the war in Europe came to an abrupt end. As part of the final treaty, the Russians took control of Eastern Europe, including Poland. The Poles of Tengeru mourned the loss of our beloved homeland, and we wept openly at the prospect of never seeing our homes or loved ones again.

The Russian-controlled communist government in Poland sent a group of representatives to Tengeru in an effort to persuade us to return with them to Poland. Everyone in the village gathered in our outdoor theater to hear the delegates deliver speeches that promised us lifelong financial security in "the new, improved people's paradise." But after suffering through years of oppression at the hands of the Russians, we trusted them about as much as a sheep farmer would trust a wolf, and the emissaries withdrew from the stage as the audience jeered and shouted, "Traitors! Traitors!"

My mother met nightly with the neighbors to discuss our options now that the war was over. We were certain my father was alive and was still in the Polish army, but we weren't sure where he was stationed or how long he would remain on active duty. My mother was set on moving from Tengeru as soon as possible because Mt. Kilimanjaro, an inactive volcano, was showing signs of re-awakening. We'd already felt the tremors from several small earthquakes, and even a small eruption could level our village in minutes.

To complicate matters, Polish soldiers were being discharged by the thousands, which meant the village's primary means of support was rapidly dwindling. The population of our village was dwindling, too, as our friends began leaving the village daily to seek new homes and build new lives. My mother thought our best option was to find a job in a nearby city and save enough money to buy a farm in Rhodesia. Whatever we finally decided about our future, one thing was for sure. We were running out of time. We had to decide where we would go and what we would do — and soon!

"Mother! Mother! Look — a letter from Papa!" I shouted, waving the letter above my head as I sped down the narrow path toward my mother, who was weeding a small garden in front of our tukula.

"It's wonderful news, mother! It's from Papa. We're going to be together again soon!"

I hugged my mother tightly as she scanned the contents. My father was still in the military, and he had received orders to report to an army base outside London. The orders stipulated that his wife and child were authorized to join him at their earliest possible convenience, at government expense!

In 1948 my mother and I packed our belongings and left Tengeru forever. The thrill of my first airplane ride was eclipsed by my excitement of our long-overdue family reunion. After six long years, we were finally going to be together again, in England. This was our chance to begin again in a country that honored and encouraged freedom. I was bursting with happiness, thinking that finally, after all our suffering and misery, our dreams had come true.

Little did I know that England was only the beginning of our dreams. As it turned out, our biggest dreams would come true in a far-away country called the United States of America.

12
A Tearful Reunion

"I'm going for a walk with the girls," I said to my mother as I headed out the door of our barracks in a military outpost near London. "We want to explore British civilization. I've already unpacked my suitcase. We won't be long, Mamma."

"Please be careful, dear," my mother replied. "And stay in your group. There's no telling what you'll find on those streets!"

I hurried to join my friends waiting outside. My mother and I had just arrived at the compound, and we were settling in, anxiously waiting for my father to contact us. I hurried across the street to meet my friends, jamming my hands into my coat pockets as I shivered slightly in the cool, damp air. It would take a while for me to adjust to this climate after Africa, I thought to myself.

Walking briskly down the street with two girl friends from Tengeru, I eagerly surveyed our new home. Compared to our village in Africa, the military base was a modern metropolis. We marveled at the buildings and stared in awe at the steady stream of army trucks and jeeps that whizzed by us. The streets were crowded with soldiers, some marching in formation, others briskly walking from one building to another while carrying arm loads of official-looking documents.

"Well, what do you think of your new home?" one of the girls asked, opening her arms wide as if to embrace the entire country.

"I haven't made up my mind yet," replied my other friend. "All we've seen so far are some old army barracks, a few buildings, and soldiers everywhere. As a matter of fact," the friend whispered as she leaned toward us, "I think we're being followed by a few soldiers right now. What do you think, Alicia?" she said as she glanced nervously behind us.

"Nonsense," I replied. "We're not in Russia anymore. Soldiers don't follow you around in England."

I looked behind me to see a small group of men engaged in a lively conversation, and I quickly decided they were too engrossed in their conversation to notice us. But as I turned back to say something to my friends, I came to a sudden stop. I felt my breath rush out of me, and my body went cold with shock.

"What's the matter, Alicia?" one of the girls asked with obvious concern. "You're as white as a sheet! Are you having another attack of malaria?"

My friends hurried to my side, hooking their arms under my elbows to support me in case I fainted.

"Dear, God," I cried as I turned back toward the approaching service men. *"It's my father!"*

I pulled away from my friends and dashed toward the soldiers, who stopped and stared as I rushed toward them with my arms extended. I singled out a tall, fair-haired soldier with a distinctive walk, and I could see his startled face break into a wide smile as soon as he recognized me.

"Alicia! It's my daughter, Alicia!" he cried, leaning forward to catch me as I leaped into his arms. I wrapped my arms around my father's neck and wept.

My father hugged me around my waist and reached up with one hand to stroke my hair, as if to reassure himself that I was real.

"I've prayed for this moment a million times," he sobbed. "My little girl is all grown up. Let me look at you, Alicia!"

We walked back to the barracks arm in arm, stopping from time to time to hug tearfully.

"Papa, Mother was right about one thing," I said haltingly between sobs. "She warned me that there was no telling what I would find on these streets!"

We laughed and hugged again before turning once more toward the barracks where my mother was waiting. As we neared our new home, we smiled at each other ... and then sprinted toward Mother's door, laughing all the way!

13

America, Land of the Free!

I f you were born in America, it would be hard NOT to take this country for granted. But I can tell you from experience that millions of people in other parts of the world don't take America for granted at all. They long for America like a thirsty man longs for water.

To the oppressed, America is justice.

To the poor, America is opportunity.

To the ignorant, America is education.

To religious minorities, America is tolerance.

But most of all, to billions of people throughout the world, America is freedom.

Freedom to shape your own destiny.

Freedom to make your own choices.

Freedom to follow your own dreams.

My family dreamed of living in America ever since our darkest days in Mala Jeluga, when we accepted the fact that the Russians would never allow Poland to regain its freedom. We longed for our home in Poland, but as long as the communists were in control, it would never be OUR home again — it would always be

THEIR home. So we did what we had to do to survive, and we dreamed of living in a country as free as America.

We stayed in London from 1948 to 1951, but for some reason, it never felt like home to us. Yes, there were things about England that we loved, like the excitement of living near London, one of the great cities of the world. And we enjoyed and admired the best of the English way of life — the everyday freedoms ... the endless traditions ... the grand history ... the ancient architecture ... the wonderful people.

We loved living in England, but it was a transitional place. The country was packed with refugees and soldiers displaced by the war, most of whom were heading to new lives in South America, Israel, and the United States.

We received a letter from a professor my mother met in Africa telling us what a marvelous country America was. Here's part of his letter:

Queens, New York
September 15, 1951
Dear Jozef and Janina,

As I promised you before my departure from London, I am writing to share with you my opinion of the United States as a possible choice for the relocation of your family.

By all means, come! Immediately! Everything we heard about this country is true. The jobs, the wealth, the limitless opportunities, FREEDOM — they all are here for the taking by those persons with the slightest bit of initiative.

Many of my associates own homes, and EVERYONE has a refrigerator — and food to put in it! Incredible, you say? That's not all. Americans do NOT mend the holes in their stockings. They buy a new pair instead!

Knowing how you value life and freedom, I urge you, my dear friends, to take advantage of your opportunity to settle in the U.S.A. It is a move you will not regret.

Your friend,
Henry

We'd dreamed of living in America, and the professor's letter was all we needed to cement our decision.

Emigrating to America

In 1951 my parents had received permission for us to emigrate to America. The voyage from England to America by ship took us a month and covered 3,000 miles. But in truth, our journey began 11 years before in a prison camp in Siberia.

Beginning with a knock on our door in Poland in 1940, we traveled 12,000 miles, much of it in cattle cars. We resided in seven different countries, most often in mud huts. And we existed on a starvation diet that was barely enough to sustain a small child, much less a family of three. But our dream of someday living in America was a candle in our darkest despair.

I can still remember as if it were yesterday that cold, fall day in 1951 when we arrived at our port of entry in St. John, Nova Scotia. I was 17 years old. My mother was in her early 40s. My father in his early 50s. Everything we owned was packed into five suitcases, and my father had $400 cash in his pockets. That's all we had to our names. Here we were, three Polish immigrants who could barely speak the language, starting over with a few hundred dollars to our names.

You'd think we would have been scared, miserable, and depressed. But we didn't think of ourselves as poor or underprivileged — not for a second! We thought we were rich! As we huddled together on the dock, stomping our feet to keep warm, we counted our blessings and celebrated like children at Christmas.

Our dream had finally come true, and we thought we were the luckiest people in the world!

We were in America!

We were free!

Chronicle of Events
The Rest of Our Story

November, 1951

After entering the country, we migrate to Queens in New York City, where the nephew of a friend lets us live in his apartment building rent-free for two weeks.

My father finds work as a landscaper and caretaker of the nursery on the estate of a well-to-do businessman in Brookfield, Connecticut. My mother also works at the estate, managing the housekeeping responsibilities and tending a greenhouse of prized orchids.

June, 1953

I finish high school in Brookfield, and in the fall I enroll in a two-year dental hygiene program at the University of Bridgeport. I graduate from the program in 1955 and immediately take a position as a dental hygienist while working on my bachelor of science degree.

1956

My parents and I become American citizens.

December 31, 1957
On New Year's Eve, 1957, I attend the Polish Merchant Marines Ball, where I am introduced to Hank Gilewicz, a young civil engineer. On May 24, 1958, we are married and settle in New York City.

January 24, 1961
Our first son, Michael, is born on the same day that Hank is hired by IBM. A year later we move to Poughkeepsie, New York, and buy our first home, an English Tudor-style house on 16 acres.

December 22, 1964
Our second son Mark is born.

January, 1966
Seeking a warmer climate, Hank requests a transfer to Raleigh, North Carolina. We move to Raleigh and build our dream home on 19 acres in nearby Durham. I become involved in local civic, religious, and political activities, and I am instrumental in organizing the Durham chapter of the Young Americans for Freedom. I campaign actively for Senator Jesse Helms and begin receiving invitations from all over the country to speak and share my experiences during the war. As a result of my efforts to promote freedom, I am voted Republican Woman of the Year in 1966.

1972
Hank and I sign up as distributors with the Amway Corporation.

1977
Working part-time, we become Diamond Directs within five years. Hank resigns from IBM to devote more time to our Amway business. My aging parents, Joseph, 77, and Janina, 67, share our vacation home in the mountains.

1986
We move to our current home, a one-acre waterfront home on Lake Wylie, just outside Charlotte, North Carolina.

1991

The Amway Corporation expands into Poland in 1992. Hank, our son Mark, and I return to my homeland to show the Polish people how they can become financially free through the Amway opportunity.

1992

My father passes away at age 92.

1998

My mother celebrates her 88th birthday. Mark is assuming a larger role in our Amway business, and we travel to Poland and other countries several times a year to support our growing organization.

Section 2
10 Lessons In Freedom

Lesson 1:
Dream Big Dreams

There is a giant asleep within every man.
When the giant awakes, miracles happen.
— B.C. Forbes

My childhood is a testimony to the power of dreaming big dreams. The communists may have succeeded in imprisoning me physically in a remote Siberian slave-labor camp, but their barbed wire fences couldn't contain my dreams of freedom.

When I stood in the soup line in subzero temperatures, I'd dream of the day when my family would outsmart the stone-faced guards, jump the tangled barbed wire fences, and make our way to freedom. When my stomach was burning with hunger, I would dream of freedom. When I laid my head down on a cold, wooden bench at night, I would dream of freedom.

It wasn't until many years later, after we had reached America, and I had spoken to thousands of people about the gift of freedom and free enterprise, that I fully realized what a powerful force my early dreams had on my life. I'm convinced it was those early childhood dreams that fueled my adult ambitions and my resolve when things got tough.

Everybody Has a Dream

I've never known anyone who didn't have a dream. Everybody dreams. The biggest difference between successful people and unsuccessful people is the size and scope of their dreams and the desire to see them become reality. As Dexter Yager points out in his best-selling book, *Don't Let Anybody Steal Your Dream*, "Our lives are shaped by dreams. What and where we are today is the result of dreams come true."

If my family's dream had been to survive in Russia, guess where we'd have ended up living? That's right, Russia. But our dream was bigger than that. We didn't just dream of survival — *we dreamed of freedom!* Because all of our decisions were based on becoming free, we ended up escaping from the Land of the Dead, making our way into Iran and Africa, and eventually emigrating to the "Land of the Free," the United States of America. We are proof that "our lives are shaped by our dreams."

That's why I encourage people to expand the size of their dreams. Big dreams make people reach for more. Big dreams expand people's horizons. Instead of dreaming about living in a three-bedroom house in town, why not dream about owning a five-bedroom house on the lake? Instead of dreaming about earning an extra $1,000 a month working part-time, why not dream of earning $10,000 a month working full-time?

What Size Is Your Dream?

My husband, Hank, likes to compare the size of peoples' dreams to growing pumpkins. If you take the flowers on a new pumpkin vine and stick them into quart-sized glass bottles, you will grow quart-sized pumpkins every, single time! But what do you think happens when you place the vines inside gallon bottles? That's right — you grow gallon pumpkins.

Well, people are like pumpkins and our dreams are like the glass containers that surround us. People with quart-sized dreams will never grow to become gallon-sized people because they have built their own "glass ceiling," so to speak. It's like Francis Martin says in his book *Hung by the Tongue*: "You cannot rise above what you allow yourself to think or say."

But what do you think happens when you teach people to grow bigger pumpkins by breaking their quart-size thinking and replacing it with gallon-size thinking? Or even 10-gallon-size thinking? Or how about aquarium-size thinking? Then people's pumpkins would be free to grow to their full, God-given potential, isn't that true?

Like I said earlier, there's no way my family and I could have made it to this country without a big, compelling dream — just as there's no way that Hank and I would have succeeded in the business without a big, compelling dream!

Our Dream for Poland

When the Amway Corporation announced they were going to open Poland in 1992, Hank and I sat down and had a serious talk. I'd always dreamed of returning to a free Poland and helping the Polish people realize their long-suppressed dreams by introducing them to the business. This was the opportunity of a lifetime!

But Hank and I had to face some tough realities. We were both nearing 60 years of age, and my mother, who is now 88, had suffered a stroke and needed constant attention. There were so many huge obstacles to overcome: First and foremost, the financial investment would be enormous. We had to cover travel and office expenses, legal fees, long-distance phone calls, rental costs for meeting rooms, to name a few costs.

To complicate matters, the average Polish citizen was earning about $200 a month, which meant there would be very little disposable income to buy products. When we first started working the business in Poland, most Poles didn't even have phones, much less cars, although the situation has improved dramatically over the last six years.

The outlook was bleak, to say the least, and, frankly, we didn't need the money (and we weren't at all sure there was enough money circulating to make the endeavor worthwhile). If we were looking for reasons NOT to open the business in Poland, we had a long list of them.

But I couldn't ignore or deny my dream of someday introducing the business to Poland. You see, my dream for Poland wasn't about what was best for my family. Hank and I had already accomplished our financial dreams. My dream for Poland wasn't about financial freedom and independence FOR US. It was about what we could do FOR OTHERS.

We decided to follow our dream and share the business with the Polish people.

Rebuilding the Walls of Jerusalem

Several months before our scheduled flight to Poland, I woke up one night in a panic thinking of everything that had to be done. I was overwhelmed.

"There's no way we can get everything done in time," I told Hank. "This is overwhelming."

"Great dreams take great preparation," Hank responded calmly. If your dream is big enough, the facts don't matter. Our dream is big enough, Alicia. We can make this work. We will make this work."

Hank and I prayed and asked God to give us the strength to continue and to triumph. We were inspired by the Old Testament story of Nehemiah, who prayed for four months and then rebuilt the walls of Jerusalem in 52 days. This story shows what can happen when preparation is combined with prayer.

Well, I'm delighted to report that the opening of Poland was a resounding success! The Poles were quick to grasp the concept of networking, so much so that Poland set a record for the fastest start of any Amway market in the world! Within the first year, 100,000 people had signed up in the business!

Now that our dreams are starting to materialize in Poland, we can see even greater things ahead, and we are expanding our dreams daily. In our private moments we talk about touching the lives of people in every town in Poland — a nation of 39 million people. Our dream includes establishing an outreach to prisoners, working with students on university campuses, supporting orphanages, running a youth leadership camp, and building churches.

Without a big dream, Hank, Mark, and I would be sitting on our front porch congratulating ourselves for having the good sense to stay away from Poland and all of its "insurmountable" problems.

But our dream carried us above the negatives. Our dream softened the hard realities. And today I'm proud to say that we are sharing our dream of freedom with tens of thousands of Poles who had been denied freedom for half a century. And they are sharing it with their friends and loved ones, not only in Poland but throughout the world.

Keep Your Eyes on the Prize

Sadly, most people don't allow themselves to dream big dreams. Hank always says that most people live their lives backward because they let their income limit the size of their dreams, instead of allowing their dreams to determine what their income can become.

That's why, all too often, people with pint-sized incomes have pint-sized dreams. If people would allow themselves to dream big dreams and then place those dreams out in front of their lives, they'd start working at opportunities that would empower them to break free from their self-imposed limitations.

Hank and I are a good example. Our dream was to break free of the corporate world, where Hank's boss and the company had complete power over our lives. We dreamed of owning our own business and becoming financially free within five years. When times got rough, we looked past the temporary obstacles and focused on the big picture — our dream of total financial freedom. Our dream is what kept us moving forward, no matter what.

It's like swimming the English Channel, a cold, current-swept, 21-mile-wide stretch between England and France. If every swimmer had given up every time he or she got stung by a jellyfish or suffered a cramp, no one would have made it to the other side.

But the successful swimmers understood that you have to *keep your eyes on the big prize at the end, not on the little wave right in front of you*. Likewise, you have to have a dream big enough and important enough that it motivates you to keep on moving forward in your life, one stroke at a time.

Beware the Dream-Stealers

Years ago I heard about a convict who was awaiting execution on death row. A visitor noticed that the condemned man had a large tattoo on his arm that read, "Born to Lose."

103

"When did you get your 'Born to Lose' tattoo" ?" the visitor asked.

"I don't remember," replied the condemned man solemnly. *"But BORN TO LOSE was written on my mind long before it was written on my arm."*

Sadly, there are a lot of people like the condemned man who have such little regard for themselves that they are seemingly incapable of big dreams. Fortunately, only a small minority of people are filled with as much self-contempt as the convict. But it seems like most people are so lacking in self-confidence that they act as if they have "Born to Be Mediocre" tattooed onto their minds. They have made settling for less their life's mission.

You've heard the expression "Misery loves company," haven't you? Well, mediocrity loves company, too. In fact, mediocre people resent anyone who tries to break away from the pack by daring to dream big dreams. They will tell you that dreaming is a waste of time. That you're bound to fail. That "these things never work."

In the business we call these mentally mediocre people "dream-stealers." They don't want you to dream big dreams because they're secretly afraid you might accomplish those dreams, which would only remind them of their own mediocrity. So they try to cut you off at the pass by discouraging you from dreaming in the first place.

Beware the dream-stealers! They are filled with fear and envy, and their goal in life is to keep others from rising above their station in life. Like I said, mediocrity loves company! David Schwartz, author of *The Magic of Thinking Big*, has this to say about dream-stealers:

"The next time someone tells you that you are foolish to dream, analyze that person, and you'll probably find that he or she is mediocre, achieving next to nothing, unadmired, and not the kind of person you would like to be."

Does this sound like someone you would like to emulate? Of course not! The goal of communism was to eliminate the elite by reducing everyone to the level of mediocrity. That's why they tried to erase people's dreams and replace them with dreary slogans about the "workers' paradise."

I didn't buy their slogans when I was seven years old, and I'm not buying it today. Communism seeks to stifle dreams by drag-

ging everyone down into the mud-pit of mediocrity. Free enterprise, on the other hand, challenges everyone to dream big dreams
and reach high for the branch of excellence.

Opportunity Is at Your Door Step

When I think of all the opportunities available in this great, big
world of ours, it breaks my heart to see people settling for less
than they deserve. It was only a few years ago that 80 percent of
the world's population lived in underdeveloped countries. But
today 80 percent of the world's population is served by the Amway
Corporation, which means the vast majority of people in this world
have an opportunity to dream as big as they want.

I've seen what happens when people wake up and start taking
advantage of opportunities. Secretaries with high school diplo-
mas take college courses at night and then go on to graduate from
law school. Sons of iron workers work their way through medical
school. College dropouts build billion-dollar software companies.
And thousands of dissatisfied, unfulfilled workers from all back-
grounds realize their biggest dreams by building large, profitable
distributorships.

Folks, right now, right this minute, is the time to start dreaming your biggest dreams. I tell you, you have what it takes to
become financially free, but you have to start dreaming like you're
financially free before you can start living like you are! And there's
never been a better vehicle than networking to make your dreams
come true.

So do what successful people do — dream big dreams, tuck
your fears and your excuses in your back pocket, and get to work
making your dreams come true!

Lesson 2:
Face Down Your Fears

> *Death is not the greatest loss in life.*
> *The greatest loss is what dies inside of us*
> *while we live.*
>
> — Norman Cousins

Several years ago I listened to a motivational speaker talking about overcoming fears. He said that fear was basically an illusion, and that in order to overcome fear, we should start thinking of each letter of the word FEAR as an acronym for this phrase: False Evidence Appearing Real.

I think what the speaker really meant to say is that many of our daily anxieties are false, which is pretty accurate. But as far as fear being an illusion, he wasn't even close.

Your Fears Are Real

Fear isn't an illusion, I assure you. You don't overcome your fears by ignoring them or passing them off as illusions. The only way to manage your fears is to *admit they are there, and then to look them in the eye and face them down.* The best way to explain what I mean is to tell you about two major events in my life where I experienced two very real, but very different, kinds of fear.

The first story involves physical fear, and it happened to my mother and me as we were trying to escape from Uzbekistan, the Land of the Dead. My mother and I were living in the mud hut with Mrs. L after my father enlisted in the Polish army, barely surviving by foraging for edible plants and digging roots out of the rocky soil.

One afternoon we received a brief letter from my father insisting that we were to join him immediately in Kerminech, an industrial city several hundred miles to the south. My mother scanned the note, and then, without so much as a hesitation, rushed us out the door to the train station. When we arrived at the station, we soon discovered that the trains had been commandeered by the army to transport military personnel and supplies. We were told that unauthorized civilians were not allowed on board.

"It's impossible for a civilian to travel on this train," the station master told my mother.

"Impossible? Well, we'll see about that!" she muttered over and over as we splashed our way back to our hut. "There are two things that station master can be sure of," she said firmly. "One is that there is a way for us to get on that train. The second is that I will find it!"

Mother made a bee-line to our suitcase and carefully removed the green silk fabric she had been holding onto. She smoothed the shimmering cloth with her hands, announcing, "Ladies, you are looking at our transportation to Kerminech!"

Just as my mother anticipated, the station master's wife found the silk cloth irresistible, and she quickly agreed to talk to her husband. Within the week we received a message to meet at the train station.

After the train chugged away from the station, the engineer instructed us to mingle with the rest of the passengers and act as if we were the family of a Red officer. As we made our way down the aisle, a burly Russian conductor planted himself in our path.

"What are you doing aboard this train?" he demanded. "This is for army only."

"Oh," my mother calmly replied in fluent Russian. "My husband is an officer, and we are traveling with him to Kerminech."

The conductor looked at us suspiciously before stepping aside. We quickly made our way through the swaying train until we found an unoccupied corner, where we stayed for the remainder of the 24-hour trip.

Don't Give in to Fear

As I look back on that episode, I marvel at how my mother faced down her fears. First of all, she refused to take "no" for an answer. If she had given in to fear and missed an opportunity to get on the train, we surely would have starved to death. And if she had panicked and blown our cover when we were questioned by the conductor, I wouldn't be sitting here writing this story, that's for certain.

Was my mother scared? Of course she was scared! In our private moments she would wring her hands and cry, and she prayed incessantly. But my mother knew that wishful thinking wouldn't make our dire situation go away. She had to make it go away by facing down her fears and taking immediate action.

Fear of Rejection

The second event happened to me when I was in my late '30s, and it represents a major turning point in my adult life. Although this second confrontation with fear wasn't a life-and-death situation, it exposed me to a fear that all of us face from time to time — the fear of rejection.

Hank and I had just signed up as distributors, and we were excited and skeptical at the same time. One of my concerns was whether or not anyone would want to buy the products, so I decided to see for myself. I called up four of my best friends and made appointments to drop by their houses the next day.

Now, before I continue, let me fill you in on some crucial background information. When we first joined the business, Hank was a veteran engineer with IBM, and I was very active and visible in the community. I was president of the local Republican Party and a much-sought-after keynote speaker for community and political organizations. As a result, my name was frequently in the newspaper, usually accompanied by a photograph of me shaking hands with a politician or civic leader.

We lived in an exclusive section of Durham and belonged to a ritzy country club. We weren't wealthy, but we were upper middle class, and many of our acquaintances were upper class, and a few were out-and-out rich. The last thing I wanted to do was embarrass myself in front of my friends.

The day of the appointments I gathered up a few cleaning products — in 1972, Amway only offered 120 products, most of which were cleaning supplies — and tossed them into my black presentation case. (The business back then doesn't compare to the business today, where we distribute almost 10,000 different products and services from more than 1,200 major corporations). Then I headed out the door for my first appointment with the wife of a prominent dentist.

I walked up to the front door of this huge, lovely home on a golf course, and the closer I got, the more afraid I got. I slipped the product carrying case under my coat and stood staring at the front door, frozen with fear.

What are you doing, Alicia? Are you out of your mind? I asked myself.

Here you are, Alicia, I said to myself, *standing on the front porch of a magnificent home, holding a case of cleaning products that you don't know anything about. Maybe this woman will think Hank lost his job. I feel like a maid. This is awful!*

My fears flooded over me from every direction:

I was afraid of what my friends would think of me.

I was afraid that no one would like the products.

I was afraid that this business was some kind of door-to-door gimmick that Hank and I had fallen for.

I was afraid of embarrassing myself.

I was afraid of failure.

I was afraid I wouldn't know what to say.

I was just one big knotted up ball of fear!

I must have stood on this woman's porch for 10 minutes, fighting this tug of war with myself. Yes ... no ... yes ... no ... yes. I was so scared, so afraid, so conflicted, that tears were welling up in my eyes.

Breaking Through My Wall of Fear

If you don't ring this doorbell right now, I said to myself, *you will never ring a doorbell. You and Hank will be slaves all of your lives, Alicia. You will never be free if you don't go through this door. Hank will be trapped in that job working for a boss who has total control over your lives. If you can't push the doorbell for yourself, Alicia, then push it for your family!*

With a burst of courage, I pressed my finger on the doorbell and hugged my black product case with both arms. It was one of the hardest things I have ever done in my life — and, as it turns out, one of the best!

To make a long story short, the woman was very gracious. She just smiled and nodded her head as I stammered about the products. Before I knew it, we were in her bathtub, scrubbing at a stubborn stain with *Re-Do*. Lo and behold, the stain came out! The product worked! I tell you, I was more delighted than my friend!

I ended up taking a $40 order that morning. It was my first sale.

You know, after that terrifying ordeal, everything else in this business has been much easier by comparison. After that day, I threw my total support behind Hank, and five years later, we reached our goal of Diamond Direct, even though Hank was still employed full-time by IBM!

Your Dreams Must Be Stronger Than Your Fears

When I stood frozen with fear on that woman's front porch 26 years ago, the dream of freedom was the motivating force that gave me the courage to push that first doorbell! I just knew in my heart that in order for Hank and me to become personally and financially free, I had to face my fears, master them, and move forward.

As I stood staring at that doorbell, I understood that I wasn't making a choice between whether or not to ring a doorbell. I was making a choice between slavery and freedom.

Without my dream, I don't think I would have had the courage to push that doorbell. But my dream gave me the courage to face down my fears. Whenever I was tempted to give in to my fears and walk back to my car, a beautiful old Polish folk song about a long-ago war would start playing in my mind:

> *They fought for freedom and lost.*
> *The wind is blowing, shaking the leaves,*
> *Scattering the ashes of their dreams.*

As I stood on that porch years ago, the plaintive melody and mournful lyrics played over and over in my head, and I could imagine my dreams of freedom turning to ashes. The image of the wind scattering the ashes of my dreams was so vivid, so terrifying, that it compelled me to face my fears and gave me the courage to act.

I didn't know it at the time, but when I pressed that doorbell years ago and the door swung open to welcome me in, I wasn't just entering the door of a friend's house. I was entering a door that would change my family's life forever.

I was finally entering the door to total freedom

Lesson 3:
Faith Can Change Your Life

Fear knocked on the door.
Faith answered.
No one was there.

— Anonymous

As I look back on my years struggling to survive in a Russian slave-labor camp ... watching in horror at the age of seven as children my age slowly starved to death ... alone and lost at the age of eight, wandering shoeless through the streets of Tehran in tattered underwear ... sick and terrifyingly alone at sea, a passenger on a ship of strangers heading to an unknown land ... alone and unloved at the age of nine on the African continent, always hungry, always sad, I'm amazed I survived.

I remember thinking to myself as I cried myself to sleep on hard dirt floors: *God, where are you? Please help me! Can you hear me, God? Please answer me. God, where are you?*

What About Your Struggles?
Most of my early life I was asking, "Is life worth living?" Every

113

day would bring more struggles, more misery, more heavy, dark clouds of despair: *I'm drowning, God! God, are you there? Do you hear my cries in the night? I don't know the answers, God. Give me a sign. God, where are you?*

Maybe you've felt the way I felt during my days in the wilderness — struggling to get through your day, asking questions but never getting any answers. Miserable. Desperate. Angry. And alone. So, so alone.

Our Story

Years later, even though I was happily married and enjoying a privileged life-style, I was still asking the same question — *"God, where are you?"* I had a beautiful home. I was married to a successful engineer and belonged to an exclusive country club. I was surrounded by devoted friends and a loving family. But deep down inside, I still felt alone. I was still longing for God.

Hank was searching for answers, too, so I wasn't alone in my spiritual quest. Was God always important to me? Yes. Have I always searched for Him? Yes. The same was true for Hank. We went to church every week, and we had an awesome respect for God, but we didn't really know Him. We were never encouraged to study scripture for ourselves, and we had no idea what it meant to have a personal relationship with the Lord.

The Bible was a holy book to us, but we didn't ever think of it as a "living" testament. We knew something was missing in our relationship with God — we just didn't know what to do about it.

After we had been in the business for several months, we attended a major weekend function. At many major events, an optional non-denominational Sunday service is made available because people are away from their home church. On Sunday morning I said to Hank, "Why don't we visit the Sunday service? Let's see what it's all about."

We sat through the service in total amazement! People were talking about Jesus as if they knew him intimately. They sang songs of praise from their hearts — not from a hymn book. It was as if the word of God was personal, and the worshipers understood it.

Why was I never exposed to this before, I thought. Mixed emotions swept over me like a flash flood. I was shocked by the unbridled outpouring of emotions ... I was overjoyed to discover that people could feel this way about God ... yet I was disappointed that I had never had the opportunity to see God in this new light.

It broke my heart to know that for my entire life, Jesus was there, right in front of me, but I never knew Him. Much of my life had been such a struggle. What a difference it would have made if I had known Him!

Committing Ourselves to the Lord and to the Business
Hank and I started attending the Sunday services at every major function. We absorbed the music and the Bible messages like a thirsty sponge. The more we heard, the more we wanted to hear, and we began to study God's word.

At home we began watching the televised crusades of Billy Graham. We were moved by the great love he had for Jesus, and Mark and I would often kneel down to pray as Billy Graham encouraged us to open our hearts so that Jesus could enter. Billy Graham's sermons sounded wonderful, but we didn't understand the true meaning of his words. We were so full of religion and ritual that we knew nothing of what it meant to have a personal relationship with Jesus Christ. We didn't understand that salvation comes through Jesus' sacrifice on the cross and His grace, and that it had nothing to do with our good works.

Then, in December of 1973, during the Sunday service following a Dream Weekend at the historic Grove Park Inn in Asheville, North Carolina, the guest pastor said something that Hank and I were ready to hear.

"If you are ready to accept Jesus as your personal Savior," he pronounced, "please come forward so that we can pray with you."

Hank and I took a bold step of faith, and we ran to the front of the auditorium, where the minister shared this scripture: "For God so loved the world that He gave his only begotten Son, that whosoever believes in Him shall not perish but have everlasting life."

When I asked Christ to forgive me of my sins, it was as if a dam had broken within me! I cried tears of repentance and joy and felt total freedom. Not even being released from Mala Jeluga could compare to this feeling.

Later that day Hank said to me, "Alicia, we are going to build a business together that we will be proud of. Now we have a senior partner in our business," Hank continued, "who has promised us that 'If we do the work, He will perform the miracles.' I will see to it that we do our part."

Right then and there we made a commitment that everything we did from that moment on would combine faith and action.

What Is Faith?

Faith doesn't always come easily. Sometimes it takes years of searching, which was the case with Hank and me. Oh, sure, it's easy to believe when you're holding something tangible in your hands. But the Bible defines faith as an intangible — "the substance of things hoped for, the evidence of things not seen."

Believing in an intangible is a whole different matter. Having faith means you commit yourself to a concept, and that's not easy. But when you finally take that leap, suddenly you can see the unseen and believe with all your heart things that have not yet occurred. And that's an awesome power to possess!

People who believe they can build their future by themselves are mistaken. We should never hesitate to turn to God for assistance in every part of our lives. Philippians 4:13 tells us to turn to the Lord for support in times of trouble with these words: "I can do everything through Him who gives me strength."

The Source of Happiness

Without question, most people's lives revolve around financial wealth more than spiritual wealth. That's not to say money isn't important. It is. You can't buy a house, put your children through college, or support a charity without it.

But too many people have made money their God, and that's when they run into trouble. Hank and I respect the power of money, but we've learned that there is much more to life than the balance of our savings account.

In the New Testament, the followers of Christ were called Christians, which means "Christ-like." Unfortunately, many people who call themselves Christians only give lip service to the powerful truth behind scripture. They have never allowed God's word to personally affect their lives.

The "rat race" cannot be won by simply running faster, and we need to escape from this hopeless treadmill. I speak from personal experience when I say that true happiness doesn't come through people or things — only through the Lord.

The Importance of Godly Principles

Hank and I have been successful in this business because we strive to build our business on Godly principles of success — honesty, integrity, love, and compassion — and we teach our people to do the same.

It should be obvious to everyone that enterprises built on the Ten Commandments will be stronger than the ones that are not. Is there anything wrong with declaring that you will not lie or steal and that you will honor your God, your parents, and your spouse? Not a chance!

It's totally impossible to keep the Ten Commandments through our own power. It takes the Lord living within us. For centuries religion has tried to improve on the Bible. But Christ is all we need. As the Apostle Paul wrote, "If you need more than Jesus, then He died for nothing."

Start Practicing the 'AS IF' Principle

Perhaps you're in the stage Hank and I were in before we took our leap of faith — searching but still unsure. "I want to believe so that God can work amazing and tremendous miracles in my life," you may be saying, "but I can't just flip a switch and turn on the light of belief. Where do I start? What do I do?"

This is the same dilemma that Hank and I faced when we first started reevaluating our relationship with the Lord. I tell people the best thing to do is to practice the AS IF principle — start acting AS IF you are a true believer, and true belief will follow.

If, for example, you are a fearful person, act AS IF you are courageous. At first this may seem foolish and impractical, but as you continue to act AS IF you were without fear, soon, to your amazement, you will discover that you are becoming courageous.

The AS IF principle is a basic mental law that changes people from what they *are* to what they *want to become*. Therefore, beginning right now, act AS IF God is with you, and strength will follow. Act AS IF you are letting go of your fears, and courage will follow. Act AS IF you are a believer, and belief will surely follow.

The Power of Belief

To believe in God and Christ and the Bible is to believe in life, in people, in goodness, and in righteousness. And finally, it is to believe in yourself as a child of God, endowed by Him with untapped potential and unused power that is waiting to be released into action.

One of the greatest "secrets" to dramatically improving your life is to stop disbelieving and to start believing. Disbelief destroys. Belief creates. Disbelief is negative. Belief is positive. Disbelief creates scarcity. Belief creates abundance.

So start practicing the AS IF principle today by having faith in God ... in yourself ... in the business ... and in life. Before you know it, your AS IF will evolve into I AM — and you will discover like so many others have discovered that faith, can, indeed, change your life!

Keep Your Eyes Heavenward and Forward

There is no reason to look back. You have to put your past behind you and move forward, which can be hard if you had a tough childhood, like Hank and I had. Or if you are surrounded with a lot of negativity from your friends and family.

My father, for example, was anything but an optimist. He never did understand the business, even after we became Diamonds. Fortunately, my mother balanced the scales. She often motivated me by saying, "Alicia, reach where your eyes cannot see." She was telling me to look at the world through the eyes of faith, to keep my eyes toward the future and heaven, rather than dwelling on past failures.

Ezra Taft Benson, an influential cabinet member during Franklin D. Roosevelt's administration, describes the power of faith with this startling image: "The Lord works from the inside out. The world works from the outside in. The world would take people out of the slums. Christ takes the slums out of people, and then they take themselves out of the slums."

Our "slums" are made up of our sins. When we accept the Lord as our personal savior, we're giving God permission to work a miracle "from the inside out" by removing the slums from our lives. Once that happens, we open the door for faith to enter and change our lives forever, just as Jesus promises in Mark 9:23:

Everything is possible for him who believes.

Lesson 4:
Learn to Lead

> *Leadership, like swimming,*
> *cannot be learned by reading about it.*
> —Henry Mintzberg,
> management expert

Dwight Eisenhower was one of the great leaders of the 20th century, first as a general heading up the Normandy Invasion during WW II, and later as 34th president of the United States.

When asked to explain his philosophy of leadership, Eisenhower would reach into his pants pocket and remove a piece of string. He'd lay the string on his desk and then ask the questioner to move the string, first by pushing it, then by pulling it.

"That piece of string illustrates the main principle of leadership," Eisenhower would say with a twinkle in his eye. "Push the string and you can barely get it to move. *But pull the string, and it will follow you anywhere.*"

This simple illustration drives home a powerful principle, namely, that true leaders are out in front of the pack, leading by example, pulling their followers behind them. As the great American philosopher Ralph Waldo Emerson put it, "What *you are* thunders so loud that I can't hear what *you say*."

You Can Learn to Lead

We've all heard the expression, "Leaders are born, not made." That's not entirely accurate. The expression should be, "Leaders are born *and* made." The truth is we're all born with leadership potential. But it remains nothing more than potential until we start putting it to use.

Even the greatest leaders in history started out as followers — we all do. When you were a child, who did the leading, you or your parents? What about when you entered your freshman year of high school — who were the leaders, the seniors or the freshmen? Same with college ... the military ... your first job ... and on and on.

Then gradually *we learn to become leaders* through education and training ... observation ... motivation ... trial and error ... research ... and experience.

Common sense tells us that all leaders must assume the role of the student before they graduate to the role of the teacher. Some may do it sooner than others, but the sequence always remains the same. Before you teach, you must learn. Before you lead, you must follow.

Low-Paid Intern to High-Paid Mentor

The concept of learning to lead is especially important in our business because duplication is the key to building a large distributorship. Your success depends on your ability to learn and work the system while teaching others to do the same.

My friend Burke Hedges calls it "Copycat Marketing 101" — you copy the leaders and then become a leader by teaching your new distributors to copy you, and so on down the line.

In a sense you start out in this business as a *low-paid intern*, but as you continue learning the business and teaching it to others, you can evolve into a *high-paid mentor*. Now, it's pretty obvious what your job as an intern entails — you have to learn everything you can about how to build your business by plugging into the proven success system of tapes, books, live events, and upline mentorship.

When it's all said and done, the key to building your business is learning to lead by evolving from a student to a mentor. Never forget that this is a people business, first and foremost, and you have to sponsor and develop people through mentoring before you can grow your organization. When I think of the great mentors in our business, I'm reminded of what Katherine Hepburn said about Spencer Tracy when someone asked her why she was so devoted to Tracy, who was, by all accounts, a very troubled and difficult man:

"He grew me up past my potential," she said humbly. "And for that I am eternally grateful." I can think of no better definition of a master mentor than a leader who "grows people up past their potential." That's exactly what the business has done for us — it's forced us to grow beyond our potential and forced us to mentor others so that they do the same.

The Mentor Mentality

What you look for in a mentor is the same thing your followers will look for in you — and what their followers will look for in them.

You're looking for people with traits you admire. You're looking for qualities that you'll want to make a part of your own arsenal of winning behavior. You're looking for positive people who will inspire you to reach for new heights. You're looking for people with strong values and deep, abiding faith. You're looking for a winner who can pass the baton to you so that you can pass it on to your people.

In short, you're looking for a person of character, someone who exemplifies integrity, honesty, compassion, dependability, loyalty, team building, and who encourages and uplifts others.

In the end, people choose whether or not to use their leadership potential. As Napoleon put it, "Every private in my army has an officer's baton in his knapsack." Napoleon was saying that all of his soldiers, even the lowest-ranking private, had the potential to become a leader. But it was up to each man to reach inside his knapsack, grab the baton of leadership, and then pass it along to others.

The same is true in our business — every distributor has the opportunity to become a Diamond if he or she makes the decision and follows through with commitment, determination, and action.

Become a Leader with Character

I'll be the first to tell you that leadership comes with a tremendous responsibility. It's not enough to light the path for people to follow — you have to make sure you're taking them on the *right path*, which is not necessarily the same as the *easy path*.

No one would question that Stalin and Hitler were leaders, but they were unprincipled tyrants who led their followers down a path of hate and intolerance, and millions of gullible followers died as a result.

That's why you will hear so many of the Amway leaders talk about "old-fashioned" values like integrity and honesty and the Golden Rule. They understand that networking is a "monkey see, monkey do" business, and if the followers see the leaders behaving unethically, they are likely to do the same.

I can't emphasize enough the role that strong character plays in building a large, long-lasting distributorship. It's the cornerstone. Arthur Friedman captured the importance of leadership when he made this observation:

Men of genius are admired.
Men of wealth are envied.
Men of power are feared.
But only men of character are trusted.

As a mentor and a leader, you must inspire trust and confidence among your people. In traditional businesses, an unethical boss holds power over you because he or she controls your paycheck. But in networking, you are heading up a group of independent contractors. And if they perceive that you are lacking in character and integrity, you'll be hard pressed to keep your organization together.

When You Lead, Others Will Follow

When John F. Kennedy announced in 1961 that the U.S. would send a person safely to the moon, the media ridiculed him as being unrealistic. His own science advisors backed away from his proclamation, saying that they had no idea how to accomplish such a feat.

"Now that the vision is in place," Kennedy responded to his critics, "we will find the answers." Kennedy, you see, understood the role of a leader. He raised the bar on people's expectations, and he refused to take "no" for an answer. Kennedy didn't live to see his dream accomplished, but his daring vision lived on long after his death.

Every effective leader accepts the responsibility of setting the agenda. It's better to set an agenda that makes people stretch and extend themselves, rather than one that is too easy. As a wise man once said, "The best way to predict the future is to create it." The effective leaders of the world aren't content to predict their future by creating a mediocre world. They seek to create a world of excellence. They seek to stretch the boundaries ... to reach for the stars ... and to inspire their followers to greater achievements than they ever dreamed possible.

Your Actions Cause Ripples

In networking, your actions may affect far more people than just yourself. (That's why it's so important to counsel upline before making big decisions.)

What happens when you throw a pebble into a pond? First there is a small splash. Then the center of the splash begins to expand into a series of ever-widening concentric circles that are a hundred times bigger than the initial splash.

The same thing happens with a leader's actions. If your actions are positive for the group, it sends out positive vibrations that ripple throughout the organization, creating even more positive actions. Conversely, negative actions create negative ripples, and the results can be disastrous.

Tapping into Your Leadership Potential

Hank and I are living proof that leadership can be developed. Before joining the business, we had always assumed leadership roles — me in the community, Hank at work — but we were only using a small part of our leadership abilities. The business forced us to exploit our full leadership potential.

Many of the top leaders in Amway weren't using their leadership abilities before they got into the business. More than likely they were stuck in jobs that required them to follow instead of lead, so they never got a chance to demonstrate their leadership abilities. That's one of the great benefits of the business — it forces people to grow and use talents they didn't know they had. I've seen it happen to thousands of people over the years.

Like I always tell people, "If we can do it, so can you." We aren't special people — we just had a special dream of becoming financially free. If we can grow as leaders, so can you. If we can build a Diamond distributorship, so can you. But you don't grow your business by sitting around talking about it. You grow it by doing the business. You grow as a person through action, not through talk.

Likewise, you learn to lead by doing what leaders do, even if your first attempts are awkward and uncomfortable. Always remember: It's not where you start that counts. It's where you finish.

As a wise man once said,
    In order to be great, first you have to be good.
    In order to be good, first you have to be bad.
    And in order to be bad, first you have to try.

Lesson 5:
Never, Never Surrender

*Our greatest glory is not in never falling,
but in rising up every time we fall.*
— Ralph Waldo Emerson

"*Sometimes, Alicia, it's easier to die than to go on living.*"
I remember my mother making that statement when we were on the verge of starving to death in the Land of the Dead. It was certainly easier to die than to go on enduring the bitter cold ... the constant hunger ... and the relentless misery.

Quitting Is NOT an Option

But no matter how miserable my parents and I were, we never considered giving up or giving in. We talked about the constant, gnawing hunger. We talked about the constant, numbing cold. *But we never talked about giving up!*

Instead, we talked about escaping. We talked about what we would eat when we were finally free. Quitting was never an option.

As I look back on the years of misery and despair that my parents and I endured, I often wonder why we survived when millions of others died. I'm convinced that God had a hand in our survival, although I don't pretend to understand why we were chosen to live when so many good, innocent people perished.

But I'm also convinced that we had a hand in our survival, too. My parents never resigned themselves to living the rest of our lives under communist rule. To them, freedom was everything. They never considered the alternative. As a result, every decision we made was made with the goal of gaining our freedom.

The Power of Commitment and Action

One thing I've learned over the years is this: For the most part, successful people and failures experience an equal amount of adversity. In fact, more often than not, successful people face more and bigger obstacles than the average person. The difference is that successful people look for *reasons to succeed*, while unsuccessful people look for *reasons to fail*.

Dear Abby once wrote a column about famous people who succeeded against the odds, in her words, "persevering in the face of life's adversities to become winners." Here's a partial list of her winners:

- Raise him in abject poverty, and you have an *Abraham Lincoln*.
- Call a slow learner "retarded" and write him off as ineducable, and you have an *Albert Einstein*.
- Paralyze him with polio from the waist down when he is four, and you have the world-famous violinist *Itzhak Perlman*.
- Label him a "helpless" alcoholic, and you have *Bill Wilson*, founder of Alcoholics Anonymous.
- Tell her she's too old to start painting at 80, and you have *Grandma Moses*.
- Take a crippled child whose only home is an orphanage, and you have *James E. West*, the first CEO of the Boy Scouts of America.

What is it that empowers people like Bill Wilson or James West to triumph in the face of adversity, when so many equally talented people give in to despair? The answer, I think, can be summed up in two words: *commitment* and *action*. When people summon these two traits and apply them with all their heart and soul, almost anything is possible.

Let's take a few moments to discuss each of these traits and then look at how they can help you achieve financial and personal freedom.

Making a Commitment and Taking Action

We have a saying in the business that illustrates the power of commitment and action: "If your WHY is big enough, you'll find a HOW TO." Think about that statement for a moment. Have you ever considered your WHY for working the business? If your WHY is to earn a few hundred dollars a month for extra spending money, then you'll find out HOW TO do that, isn't that true?

But if your WHY is to control your own destiny and live a life of freedom, then you'll find out HOW TO accomplish that goal, won't you? You see, your WHY determines your level of commitment. Your HOW TO determines your plan of action. And when you combine the two, you end up with the results of your efforts. A little WHY combined with a little HOW TO will produce little results. But when you combine a BIG WHY with a BIG HOW TO, then you get big, BIG results. It's only common sense.

When my family was trapped in Russia, our WHY was freedom at any cost, and our WHY was so strong that my parents were willing to make many life-and-death choices that eventually led to our escape from the iron grip of communism.

Stack the Deck in Your Favor

My parents understood that the only way to escape from Russia was to travel in certain government-approved organizations, like the army or the orphanage in Guzary. Civilians traveling alone didn't have a chance of ever escaping. Their fate was sealed. That's why my parents joined the Polish army, and it's why my mother placed me in the orphanage.

When my father decided to join the Polish army, for example, his decision was based on our WHY. He certainly didn't want to fight on the front lines for the communist cause, even if it was against the Nazis, but he knew that by joining the army, he would increase our odds of survival.

If my father had chosen to sit and do nothing, you'd never be reading this book right now, that's for sure, because I wouldn't be alive to write it. Most likely we would have starved to death in the Land of the Dead. My father's HOW TO was to join the Polish army, which we hoped would put us in a better position to survive. It was a desperate gamble, but committing an act of desperation was certainly superior to starving to death.

Waiting Only Works in Fairy Tales

My father wasn't the only one to make life-and-death decisions in our quest for freedom. When my mother traded her silk cloth for passage on a train commandeered by the Red army, we faced immediate execution if the communists found out we were stowaways. But my mother understood that she had to ACT boldly, or we were doomed. Thousands of Polish refugees waiting at the same train station never had the opportunity to board our train. They were left behind, and most likely they starved to death.

Again, we put ourselves in a position to survive by joining sanctioned groups; by daring to ACT, we ended up boarding the last ship out of Russia sailing for Iran. From there we made our way to Africa and, eventually, to freedom in England.

Even though I was still a young child during our years in Russia, I understood that fairy tales were the only places where women in distress got rescued by waiting around for their prince to show up, like *Snow White* and *Cinderella*.

I knew that in real life all that hoping and waiting got you was more hoping and waiting. That's why I didn't protest when my mother suggested I go to live in an orphanage. I knew that desperate times called for desperate measures — that it was crucial to do whatever it takes to increase your odds of success — and I knew that taking a risk and DOING SOMETHING was better than sitting still and doing nothing.

Action Speaks Louder Than Words

God works in mysterious ways, that's for sure. I wouldn't wish my wartime experiences on anyone, but I must admit they certainly prepared me for my adult life. Looking back, the greatest lessons of my life weren't learned at a university but in the trials

I survived as a child. If there is one thing I learned from my parents during those years of misery, it's this: Commitment is crucial, but *action is everything!* Taking the bull by the horns may get you hurt, but standing there waiting for the bull to run over you will ALWAYS get you hurt.

Both of my parents took bold actions time and again, and those actions changed my life immeasurably. Their determination to take action when confronted by fear was possibly their greatest legacy to me. "Actions speak louder than words" has always been my motto, and if it weren't for my bias for action, it's unlikely that Hank and I would have achieved our freedom through the business. As Burke Hedges always says, "Ignorance on fire is better than knowledge on ice."

The good news is that all of us can summon forth commitment and action. Not all of us are born with the talent to be a concert violinist, like Itzhak Perlman. But we can *commit* ourselves to a cause, and we can *act* on that commitment just as strongly as the most talented person in the world.

Paying Your Dues

I believe that, unlike talent, we were all born with equal measures of character. It's up to each of us to tap into our hidden reservoir of character and activate the traits that can help us succeed.

I guarantee you, somewhere along the way, every successful person had to choose between giving up or going over, around, or through the obstacles in their lives. They had to reach inside and activate their hidden reserves of commitment and action. It's called paying your dues. The price of admission to the club of success isn't free, my friend, or everybody in the world would be a success, isn't that true?

Without exception, successful people choose to pay the price for victory, no matter what the cost in time or effort, rather than accept defeat. They never, never surrender.

Turning Point in Our Business

I remember the time Hank and I had to call on our reserves of commitment and action. We desperately wanted to be free — our WHY was to liberate us from Hank's boss at IBM, who had total control over the future of our family. We saw the business as a way of taking back our lives, but for various reasons, the business just wasn't working for us.

The first 20 friends we presented the opportunity to turned us down. We were devastated. I remember sitting at the kitchen table late one night with Hank, bemoaning our failure.

"Hank," I said, "maybe this thing really doesn't work after all." It seemed that all of my dreams of freedom were withering and dying right in front of me.

"I don't want to be a slave the rest of my life, Hank," I said as the tears began to flow. "Hank, it's not going to happen. We'll never be free!"

"Honey, don't worry. We'll do it," he said as he walked around the table and placed his arms around me.

"But how, Hank? How?" I implored. "I want to believe you, but how are we going to do it?"

"Alicia," he said, "we're going to do it one by one."

"What do you mean one by one?" I asked.

"It means you make one contact, and I'll make one contact," he replied. "You make one phone call, and I'll make one phone call."

Suddenly, we were a team. I knew at that moment that if I didn't work the business, he wasn't going to, either.

"We'll build our business together," Hank said firmly.

And that's when I knew in my heart we were going to be a success. You see, our problem wasn't that the business didn't work. There were success stories all over the country. The business wasn't the problem. WE were the problem.

A Lesson in Commitment and Action

That conversation was the turning point in our business. From that evening on, our business began to take off. Why? Because *we renewed our commitment*, both to the business and to each other. And because *we decided on a plan of action* that we immediately put into practice. Commitment and action — I'm telling you, they make an invincible one-two punch!

The next day we started putting our plan into action. We set a goal to become Diamonds within five years. Hank continued to work full-time at IBM, and every evening and weekend we dedicated to building our business. In a year and a half, part-time, we doubled Hank's salary at IBM. By keeping our eyes on the prize — "Five years! Only five years!" — we learned to deal with the disappointments, no matter how big, and celebrate the triumphs, no matter how small.

At the end of five years, Hank handed in his resignation letter. We've been totally free ever since. I'm not telling you this story to impress you with our achievements. I didn't write this book to brag about my life — I wrote this book to let you know what you can make of YOUR LIFE! Folks, if commitment and action can transform our business, it can transform yours, too!

We didn't discover any long-lost secret that evening 25 years ago. We didn't suddenly get lucky. All we did was to choose to succeed by committing ourselves to the business and then acting on that commitment. There were no shortcuts. No tricks of the trade. Just blinders-on commitment and all-out massive action.

Learning from Our Failures, Celebrating Our Successes

Did we have some failures along the way? Of course! But we decided early on to expect some failures because they were inevitable in any business, just as they are in life. We just made up our minds to learn from our failures and move on. We decided that nothing was going to stop us from reaching our dream.

Winston Churchill overcame scores of setbacks during his remarkable life. He had a knack of coming back from his failures until he triumphed in the end. Late in life, Churchill was asked how he remained so resilient in the face of so many failures. Churchill's reply is a study in the application of commitment and action:

> *I determined early in life that if I wanted to make something of myself, I would have to go from failure to failure enthusiastically until I've succeeded.*

Isn't that a great way to put it — "to go from failure to failure enthusiastically until I've succeeded"? The beauty of Churchill's philosophy is that it's applicable to any endeavor. His philosophy doesn't require awesome talent. Or exceptional intelligence. Or incredible amounts of money. It just requires commitment and action.

What about you? Do you want to make something of yourself, like young Winston Churchill did? Are you willing to go from failure to failure with enthusiasm?

You know, you've got what it takes to make all your dreams come true, too. Just like Winston Churchill. Just like everyone with a dream who had the courage to go after it. Just like hundreds of Diamonds all over the world. All you have to do is *commit* to your dream ... and then take daily, *productive actions* until you've succeeded. And always remember: never, never surrender!

Lesson 6:
ABCs of Goal Setting

*The have's and the have-not's
can be traced back to the
did's and the did-not's.*
— Anonymous

At about the same time that my family and I were being transported to our frozen prison in Mala Jeluga, my future husband, 10-year-old Hank Gilewicz, was walking slowly past the front window of Mr. Schwager's Hardware Store in Brooklyn, pausing to stare longingly at a pair of $3.50 Union Hardware roller skates prominently displayed in the window.

He wanted those skates more than anything else in the whole world.

"My dream was to own those skates," Hank recalled, "so that I could play street hockey with my friends. I longed for those skates. I had to have those skates. But I was lucky to get my hands on a nickel, much less the astronomical sum of $3.50."

An Early Lesson in Goal Setting
Hank didn't have the money for the skates, but he did have the

ability, and the desire, to cut hedges, mow lawns, and wash cars — for 25 cents a job.

"It didn't take me long to calculate that if I did 14 odd jobs around the neighborhood for 25 cents a job, I'd have my $3.50, and I'd be able to buy those skates," Hank said with a laugh. He went to work and dropped a quarter in his piggy bank at the completion of each job. Within a month he was the proud owner of a shiny new pair of Union Hardware roller skates.

"I learned some lifelong lessons from that early experience," Hank says today. "First of all, I learned that it's futile to be negative about the things we don't have. Instead of becoming frustrated by not owning the skates, I devised a plan whereby they could be mine. From that early success, I learned that this same principle could be applied to virtually every area of my life — that if we build on the little successes, the big successes will follow."

When Hank was 12, he used the same work-and-save plan to buy a second-hand bike for seven dollars, which enabled him to deliver newspapers and earn even more money. Hank began to understand that there's no shame in being poor — the only shame was accepting poverty when the sky's the limit for people who set goals and work hard until those goals are accomplished.

ABCs of Goal Setting & Goal Getting
The process Hank went through to acquire his roller skates is no different from what all of us must do to get what we want in life, whether it's buying new roller skates as a child or becoming financially free as an adult. We start with a dream . . . set our goals . . . work diligently . . . and then reap the rewards of our labor. I call this process the ABCs of goal setting. They are as follows:

Articulate your dreams
Bring your dream into focus by setting goals
Commit to action

Let's take a look at each one of these ABCs of goal setting in more detail so that you fully understand why goal setting is such a powerful strategy.

Articulate Your Dreams
When I say you need to *ARTICULATE YOUR DREAMS*, what I mean is you need to give yourself permission to dream again, and

then you need to validate those dreams by discussing them with others close to you, like your spouse. This step seems so obvious, but some people have a hard time admitting their dreams — such as owning a big house on several acres overlooking a lake — because they fear it will never come true. They don't want to appear foolish, so they deny they even have dreams, or they keep them bottled up inside.

What a shame! The only way you'll ever realize your dreams is to identify them and then write them down! You may not accomplish everything you dream of, but so what! If your dream list has 100 things on it and you only accomplish one, isn't that one more than you would have accomplished if you hadn't made your list? Like a friend of mine says, "If you shoot for the moon and fall short, at least you'll have succeeded in clearing the fence."

I know Direct Distributors, for example, who have been working the business for years. Their dream is to become a Diamond, but they've never gotten past Direct. Does this make them a failure? *No way!* If they are better off after joining the business, they haven't failed — they've succeeded, isn't that true?

It's Your Dream, Not Someone Else's

One other very important thing about dreams — you have to be true to your dreams. You can't dream someone else's dream and expect it to motivate you. It has to be your dream and yours alone.

It was never our dream to own a mansion or a Rolls Royce. We live in a beautiful home on a lake and always have a new Cadillac to drive. We own our home free and clear. Every time we buy a new car or boat, we pay cash. Our dreams aren't about acquiring more luxuries. Our dream is to reach down and extend a helping hand to those who need it.

Just think — I was once an "orphan" and now we have the money to help build orphanages. When I was miserable and struggling to survive in Russia, I didn't have a Bible. Now we donate hundreds of thousands of Bibles to the Word-starved citizens of Poland, Russia, and China. Because of the blessings of the business, we're able to support churches and ministries around the world. That's our dream — to share with those who haven't had the opportunities that Hank and I have had.

You see, our dream today is to share the business with people who have never experienced the many blessings of free enterprise. That's why we travel back and forth to Poland, China, and other countries several times a year. We want to "help others help themselves" through the business.

But my biggest dream has always been freedom — first for me and my family, and then for all the people who have been enslaved by communism. My dream is to see the people prosper and grow through free enterprise, and the satisfaction that I get from helping others begin to realize their dreams is far more rewarding than living in the world's most opulent mansion or owning the world's biggest diamond ring.

Have You Articulated Your Dream?

If you are having trouble articulating your dreams, the best place to start is to write down the things that you value above all else. What's most important to you — your friendships? Your family? Your career? How about a big home on lots of land? Do you want to "give back" to others? You see, what you value will tell you where you want to end up — your life's destination, if you will. Your goals will help you chart your journey.

The ironic thing about values is they control every choice we make in our lives, yet most of us spend very little time even thinking about what we really value. When you take time to assess your values, you are laying the groundwork on which to build the rest of your life.

For example, freedom has always been a dominant value in my family's life. The reason Hank and I committed ourselves to the business was for personal and financial freedom. Certainly money is important to us — I must say, I'm glad I can drive to the grocery store in a new Cadillac rather than a used Chevy. But we didn't build our business so that we could buy a new car. We built it so that we could be free — first, last, and foremost. Owning a luxury car is a nice side benefit to building a successful business, but that's not what kept us going when things got tough.

Take a few minutes to think about what it is you really and truly value in your life. Listed below are 10 categories that will help you clarify your values. I suggest you take out 10 pieces of paper and jot down five to 10 things you value under each of the following categories. When you are done, you will have taken the

first step in articulating your dreams!
1) The Business
2) Financial
3) Friends
4) Family
5) Health
6) Community
7) Spiritual
8) Recreation
9) Personal
10) Other

Bringing Your Dreams into Focus

The second step in the ABCs of goal setting is to *BRING YOUR DREAMS INTO FOCUS BY SETTING GOALS*. If a dream is your destination, then setting goals is your road map. If you wanted to travel from New York to California by car in seven days or less, for example, you wouldn't just point your car west and hope for the best, would you? Of course not. You'd buy an atlas and then chart your way across the continent, breaking your trip down into one-day segments.

The same goes with goal setting. Your destination is your dream, and your road map is your goals. In order for your goals to work for you, they must be specific, they must be measurable, and they must have a completion date. And they must always, ALWAYS be moving you forward toward your dreams.

Stay Focused on Your Dream

When we were imprisoned in Mala Jeluga, for example, we kept our eyes trained on our dream of freedom. Every time we set a short-term goal, such as my father and mother joining the Polish army ... my mother and I stowing away on a train heading south ... or boarding a ship bound for Iran or Africa, we were always making choices that would move us closer to our ultimate dream — freedom. We never waited around, hoping our dream would come to us. We were always thinking and asking and working toward the goals that would take us one step closer to freedom.

Hank and I did the same thing when we started building the

business. Because Hank was working full-time at IBM, we had to be very disciplined about how we spent our evenings and weekends. We started with a dream of becoming personally and financially free. To us that meant establishing long-term goals of owning our dream home free and clear and having enough money in the bank that we didn't have to work unless we wanted to.

We set a medium-term goal of becoming Diamond in five years. As far as Hank and I were concerned, this goal was set in stone, and all of our short-term goals were drawn up with this one, major goal in mind: *Diamond in five! Diamond in five! Diamond in five!* We talked it, we wrote it, we sang it, we lived it. And we reached Diamond Direct in five years.

Just as 10-year-old Hank broke his "big" goal of owning a pair of skates into a series of smaller goals, we did the same with our networking business. Those smaller immediate goals formed the basis for our daily, weekly, and monthly action plan, which looked like this:

Long-Term Goal
- To achieve total freedom in our work and personal lives

Medium-Term Goal
- To achieve financial freedom by becoming Diamond Directs within five years

Monthly Goals
- Help each leg to achieve *their* monthly goals
- Work with leaders in each leg to set new goals for next month

Weekly goals
- Show The Plan a minimum of six days a week
- Analyze organization chart every Saturday; decide who needs help, what kind, and then do what needs to be done

Daily Goals
- Hank and I make two new contacts a day and set up a meeting
- Call leaders in each leg to get the "pulse" on their business
- Make follow-up calls to new prospects from depth meetings
- Accomplish the major priorities on daily "to-do" list
- Show The Plan
- Make written to-do list of tomorrow's priorities

We set up three meetings every night — first a follow-up stop at the house we showed The Plan to the night before ... then the regular meeting ... and finally, we showed The Plan or closed another meeting in town to ensure good follow up.

I made it my job to call the woman the next day, and I stopped by her house for a few minutes to talk about her dreams and her fears. I left products, and if the couple got in the business, I worked with the women while Hank worked with the men. Hank and I were very aware of what was happening in our whole organization, and we worked hard to build the leaders, and we always led by example.

One of the keys to our success is that we were disciplined and totally focused on our goals. For example, we made up "signs" with our P.V. goals for the month, and we posted them all over the house to remind ourselves of our commitment. We taped our goals on the bathroom mirrors, on the refrigerator, on the kitchen table, on the rear view mirror of the car — we even had them taped to the top of the toilet seats! We were serious about accomplishing our goals!

Plan Your Work and Work Your Plan
Please understand that I'm not suggesting *our* plan of action is the best way to build *your* business. I'm sharing our goals with you because I wanted to show you what goal setting looks like. I am suggesting, however, that you sit down and put your goals down on paper — and there's no time like the present!

When I think of the power of goal setting, I'm always reminded of a speech in which our good friend Lennon Ledbetter asked the question, "How do you have a personal best year?" Here's his classic response:

How do you have a personal best year? Twelve back-to-back personal best months. How do you have a personal best month? Four back-to-back personal best weeks. How do you have a personal best week? Seven back-to-back personal best days. So wake up every morning committed to having your personal best day!

Action: Where the Rubber Meets the Road
The final letter in the ABCs of goal setting stands for *COMMIT*

TO ACTION. A wise man once said that "when it's all said and done, more is said than done." Boy, oh, boy, is that ever the truth! There's no question that it's a lot easier to talk the talk than it is to walk the walk, but until you commit yourself to making phone calls, setting up meetings, showing The Plan, and following through, you won't see any results in your business.

If someone asked me to name the single biggest shortcoming of new distributors in the business, I'd say without hesitation that it was failure to take action. The great boxing champion Joe Louis used to say, "Everybody wants to go to heaven, but nobody wants to die." Same thing with the business — everybody wants to become Diamond, but only a few people are willing to do the work.

Two Pitfalls to Taking Action

I think there are two big pitfalls that stop people from taking action — procrastination and lack of discipline. Procrastination seems innocent enough — "I'll get to it first thing tomorrow" — but tomorrow never comes. There's not much advice I can give to you if you are a chronic procrastinator except to recognize it and then DO something every time you feel the urge to put something off until another day.

I can tell you this: I've met a lot of Diamonds over the years, and they are all different. Some are organized, and some are scattered. Some are loud and some are quiet. Some are funny and some are serious. Some are brilliant and some are average. I could introduce you to a hundred Diamonds, and each one would have different strengths and different weaknesses. But I never met a Diamond who was a chronic procrastinator. NEVER!

Discipline Is Essential

The second pitfall to taking action is lack of discipline. Now, I realize that discipline is not a word that most Americans run to embrace, especially in this age of easy credit and instant gratification. But without discipline in your life, you'll never get anywhere near accomplishing your goals. That's just the hard truth of the matter.

Discipline is perhaps the single biggest reason my family was able to survive our ordeals during the war. My father was very disciplined at rationing our food and water. We witnessed scores of other families starve to death during our train rides because they failed to exercise discipline and they ran out of food.

A Tough Choice at the Doll Store

One incident during our war years especially stands out in my mind. We had just been released from Mala Jeluga, and we hitched rides on wagons, sleighs, and trucks until we arrived in the city of Kotlas. This was the first city we had visited in over two years. We walked down the main street, gazing in store windows and enjoying the hustle and bustle of a city.

I was eight years old at this time, and I remember stopping in front of a doll shop to admire a spectacular display of dolls of all shapes and sizes. I hadn't enjoyed the luxury of cradling a doll in my arms for more than two years, and my heart was melting as I stared at the hundreds of colorful dolls.

"Oh, look," I cried with delight. "They are all so beautiful. Could we buy one, Papa? Could we, please?"

"I'm sorry, Alicia, we can't buy a doll today," my father said, casting his eyes downward in shame. "We don't have even a ruble to spare. We must save all of our money for food."

"Oh, please, Papa," I cried. "I won't ask for anything else ever. Just one doll. A small one. Any one. Couldn't we just ask the price? I want a doll more than anything in the world, Papa. Please!"

"You know we don't have a single ruble to spare," my father said sternly. "Now let's go!"

I was startled by my father's tone of voice — so hard. So cold. Tears streamed down my cheeks as my father squeezed my hand harder and pulled me away from the store front.

Keep Your Eyes on the Prize

Years later my father confessed that his refusing to buy me a doll costing just a few kopeks was one of the hardest decisions he'd ever had to make, and it broke his heart to refuse a small indulgence for his only child.

My father wasn't being hard-hearted. He was being disciplined. He knew that a few rubles could buy a crust of bread or a bottle of fresh water. A few rubles could be the difference between life and death. It broke my father's heart to refuse my simple request, but by keeping his eyes trained on the big picture, he was able to make choices that would move us toward our dream of freedom.

By exercising discipline and setting goals, you, too, can achieve your dreams. But you have to be willing to make some sacrifices. Like I always say, *keep your eyes on the prize*!

I guarantee you, when you walk across the stage to accept each of your new pins (and start receiving bigger and bigger checks in the mail), you'll realize that, in the long run, the price you'll have paid for success is far cheaper than the price you'd pay for quitting.

Lesson 7:
Build Lifelong
Relationships

> *You can make more friends in
> two months by becoming interested
> in other people than you can in two years
> trying to get people interested in you.*
> — Dale Carnegie

The main reason Hank and I joined the business was to become financially free, and in that respect, the business has exceeded our expectations.

But we've enjoyed another benefit we didn't even anticipate, a benefit equally as valuable as freedom — *personal growth.* Both Hank and I have made enormous strides as people during our years in the business, and for the most part, our growth can be credited to the many wonderful, lifelong relationships that have shaped us in so many ways.

We're a Work in Progress
When you stop to think about it, who we are and what we become is little more than the sum total of our relationships with God and

with each other. Each of us is a little of this person and a little of that person. In a sense, we're all a work in progress until the day we die, and our progress is advanced, or impeded, by our relationships.

My life has been changed forever by relationships with so many wonderful, inspiring people since joining the business, and I've tried to emulate their most exceptional qualities, such as Dr. Norman Vincent Peale's warmth, sincerity, and Godliness ... Jesse Helms' determination, integrity, and statesmanship ... Rich DeVos and Jay Van Andel's belief, persistence, and commitment ... Dexter Yager's drive, leadership, and vision ... and Bill Britt's focus, passion, and patriotism.

Like I always tell people, when you try to act like a person you admire, you may not get the results they get, but you will get better as a person, that much I guarantee!

Relationships Increase Our Value

I read something the other day that really hit home. It said:

One telephone is worthless.

Two telephones begin to have value.

A network of many telephones is wealth.

This is a great observation about the way wealth will continue to be created in the "Information Age," but it's also an observation about the timeless importance of relationships. No doubt about it, our value — like the value of a telephone — increases dramatically each time we develop a strong, positive relationship with another person. A network of many relationships is wealth in the largest sense of the word — financial, spiritual, and personal.

Relationships Are Everything

Hank and I have developed so many lifelong relationships over the years that never would have been possible if he had stayed in the corporate world. Like Hank used to say, "The problem with trying to climb the corporate ladder is everybody is always stepping on your fingers."

In most business settings, you're in competition with your fellow workers. There are only a limited number of top-paying positions, and everybody is scratching and clawing their way up the corporate pyramid, which makes it hard to build great relationships.

But in networking, you get paid to help people. If someone you sponsor goes on to out-perform you, you're not envious — you're ecstatic, because the more money they make, the more money you make! Networking frees you to build deep, loving relationships that last a lifetime.

Making and nurturing lifelong relationships is the key to building a profitable networking business. This is a people business first, last, and foremost, for without people in your organization, nothing happens! Without people, no product is moved. Without people, no commissions are earned. People are the lifeblood of this business.

That's why Hank and I always tell our people, "No one cares how much you know until they know how much you care." This statement should be the slogan by which you build your business.

We All Need Each Other

When I think about the importance of relationships, I'm reminded of the story about the guest conductor of a major orchestra who was rude to all the musicians. Everyone despised him.

After enduring two weeks of constant criticism from the conductor, the orchestra assembled for the final dress rehearsal only hours before opening night. The auditorium was packed with the orchestra's friends and benefactors. The conductor raised his baton and motioned for a downbeat. Nothing happened — total silence.

The stunned conductor squared his shoulders, raised his baton once again, and gave the downbeat. Silence. Finally the first chair violinist stood up and said, "*We just wanted to show you that no sound comes out of that baton of yours.*"

This story illustrates what happens when people neglect to build relationships, especially in networking. You are like the conductor and your new distributors are like the members of the symphony. Without their cooperation, nothing happens. The only way you can coax a masterful performance out of them is to make them want to perform. That's where relationships come in. People will only perform to their potential when they think you have THEIR best interest at heart, NOT YOURS!

Years ago Ralph Waldo Emerson made this observation about relationships: "The only way to have a friend is to be one." In other words, if you practice the Golden Rule and treat others as you would like them to treat you, your relationships will flourish.

Wiser and Softer

There was a time when I acted more like the rude conductor than I would like to think. When Hank and I first started the business, I didn't have much patience with people. I've always been a "let's-get-it-done-NOW" type of person — very aggressive, very intense. I had a tendency to overdo it sometimes.

I was talking with one of our long-time distributors a while back, and she reminded me that I was very demanding in the early days of the business. At the time I didn't think I was being a slave driver. I thought the woman was a "southern belle" who wanted everything done at her convenience, which really wasn't the case. But back then I was long on ambition and short on tact, and in my determination to make the business happen, I steam-rolled over some people.

Today, I'm happy to say, Hank and I are much wiser and softer in our dealings with people. Friendships are essential and we savor each and every one of them. Just as you cherish and respect your own values, you must learn to respect other people's values, as well. Treasure others for who they are, not for who you want them to be.

Of course, you want your friends and your new distributors to grow in all areas of their lives, but you can't force people to grow according to your schedule. People have their own rhythm and style, and you have to allow them to grow and develop at their own pace. Honor your friends and business associates. Uplift them. Forgive them. Spend time with them. Learn to say, "I love you" and mean it to the depths of your soul. You'll be amazed at how people blossom when you encourage them.

Finding a Mentor

Other than your relationship with your family and God, the most important relationship you can develop in the business is to find a great mentor. The mentor's job is to coach you on the "do's and don't's" of the business. A mentor's slogan should be "Help me to help you."

Usually your first mentor will be your sponsor. Later, as you grow in the business, you may want to seek out a more knowledgeable mentor upline. If you are serious about the business, you'll find the mentor you need when you need him, one way or the other.

Hank and I had many mentors over the years, and we always sought them out, rather than waiting around for a mentor to magically appear. We were fortunate to have Dexter and Birdie Yager, whom we love and respect, as our first mentors in the business, and to this day they remain dear friends.

A word to the wise — if your sponsor is too busy (or too inexperienced) to act as your mentor, *don't use this as an excuse to quit the business!* It's up to YOU, no one else, to get the knowledge that will help you build your business. Believe me, this is one business where, if you want a good mentor, you can find one.

Becoming a Mentor

As you learn the business from a mentor, you, in turn, will become a mentor to the people in your organization. As you learn the business, you will be coaching others, teaching them the "tricks of the trade" so that they can duplicate the success of your upline Diamond.

The key to becoming a great mentor is to believe in people and to bring out the greatness in them. You need to lead people away from their limiting beliefs by gently encouraging them to begin mining their hidden potential. Don't try to create people in your own image, but rather give people the opportunity to create themselves.

Hank's speaking style, for example, is very different from mine. I'm a freedom fighter — emotional and passionate. Hank is an engineer — logical and systematic. It would be a mistake for me to insist that Hank teach and train like me. It's just not his style. One style isn't necessarily "right" and the other "wrong." Even though our styles are different, they are both effective, and that's all that counts, isn't that true? The point is that good mentors encourage their people to build on their unique strengths and talents.

The best way to lead people in this business is to lead by example. Hank and I never ask anyone to do something that we wouldn't do. We've never assumed the role of "lord of the manor" when working with our new people. Instead, our mentoring style is what I call "servant leadership." Here's the difference. The lord of the manor treats his new distributors like subordinates. He orders them around. He scolds them. He criticizes them. He evaluates them. He intimidates them. In short, he acts like a boss and treats his people like entry-level employees.

The servant leader, on the other hand, asks the question, "How can I help you become successful?" He encourages his people. He listens. He facilitates. He leads by example. He cheerleads. He recognizes and celebrates successes, no matter how big or how small. In short, he acts like a partner and coach and empowers the members of his team to accomplish more than they could on their own.

The Awesome Power of Love

If there is one, single key to building lifelong relationships, it would be this: Learn to love. I know it sounds corny, but love has the power to transform and rejuvenate relationships like nothing else.

I heard a delightful story recently about the power of love to transform lives that I'd like to share with you. It seems a woman was unhappy in her marriage and very angry at her husband. Finally, she'd had enough, and she went to her lawyer to begin divorce proceedings.

The woman was so hurt and angry with her husband that she asked her lawyer what she could do to get back at him for causing her so much misery. The lawyer thought for a moment and then came up with a brilliant plan for the ultimate revenge.

"First of all, don't tell your husband you're planning a divorce," said the lawyer. "Don't even mention to him that you visited a lawyer. When you go home, here's what I want you to do: For the next couple of months, love and romance your husband with every ounce of your being. He'll fall in love with you all over again. Then, just when he least expects it, serve him with divorce papers. It will devastate him!"

The woman agreed that this was a perfect way to get her revenge, and she headed back home with a devious smile on her face. Several months later, as scheduled, the woman re-visited the attorney.

"How'd my plan work?" asked the smiling attorney. "Are you ready to sign the divorce papers?"

"The plan worked great," the woman said, returning his smile. "In fact, it worked so well that I won't be needing those divorce papers after all. I just thought you'd like to know that we're getting ready to leave for our second honeymoon."

The More You Give, the More You Get

This story illustrates a timeless lesson — you get back what you give out. If you give out vibrations of hate and anger, that's what you get back. When you give out love, on the other hand, more often than not, you get back love in return. It's like Dr. Norman Vincent Peale's common sense observation: "Getting people to like you is the other side of liking them."

Think of it this way: Every day millions of people deposit money into a savings account. Why? So that the savings will grow, slowly but surely, until, over time, those little deposits add up to a great big investment that can provide security down the road.

Well, relationships are like savings accounts. If we make regular deposits of affection, affirmation, and positive coaching, then a relationship grows. But if we make more withdrawals than deposits, then the value of the relationship dwindles until it eventually disappears.

I can tell you from experience that when you make regular deposits in your relationship accounts, your bank accounts will start to increase also — making you richer in all areas of your life!

Lesson 8:
Integrity Begins With an "I"

*Live in such a way that
you would not be ashamed
to sell your parrot to the town gossip.*
— Will Rogers

There's a true story circulating around Russia that bears repeating because incidents like it have become common occurrences since the fall of communism. The story goes like this:

A Russian businessman importing thousands of bottles of expensive wine was detained at the port of entry by a high-ranking customs agent.

"What seems to be the problem?" the businessman asked impatiently.

"I'm sorry to say your shipment cannot enter the country without my approval," the agent said matter of factly. "But for $10,000 cash, I'll make sure your shipment is released immediately."

The businessman considered the proposition for a moment before replying, "Why would I pay you a $10,000 bribe when I could have you killed for only $2,000?" The businessman got his wine through customs without paying a penny.

Right now many Russian businessmen are still using black market tactics they learned under the old communist system, such as bribery. But as Russia grows into capitalism, they will soon learn that integrity builds trust, and trust is at the heart of every long-lasting enterprise.

You're Only as Good as Your Word

I learned early in life that you are only as good as your word. The battlefields of WWII were littered with worthless treaties and broken peace accords signed by unethical tyrants like Hitler and Stalin and Mussolini. An iron-clad contract doesn't mean anything if the person signing it has no intention of honoring it, isn't that true?

Do you remember when Ronald Reagan referred to the Soviet Union as "the Evil Empire"? He caught a lot of flak from the press about that comment, but all he was doing was voicing the truth! The fact is the entire communist system was built on lies ... falsehoods ... corruption ... favoritism . . . intolerance ... the list goes on and on. If building a system of government around immoral principles isn't evil, I don't know what is!

Forced Confession

I remember the day my father was called into the commandant's office when we were imprisoned in Mala Jeluga. The commandant insisted my father sign some papers that he wasn't even allowed to read.

"Dabrowski!" shouted a red-faced KGB agent. "Sign these papers at once!" It was common knowledge among the workers that prisoners who refused to sign were immediately taken outside and shot through the base of the skull.

Powerless, my father did as he was told, and as he scribbled his name, he furtively scanned the papers to discover the bogus charges that could some day be used against him. As best as he could figure, he had just signed a document confessing he was a capitalist spy and, therefore, could be executed as a traitor at a moment's notice.

This was the communist's idea of justice — the state could do no wrong. In the communist system, might makes right. And the state has all the might.

The Golden Rules of Business

Now compare the Russian version of conducting business with J.C. Penney's "Golden Rules" of commerce. Penney, by the way, founded thousands of stores all over North America, and in the process, became one of the richest, and most respected, businessmen in the world. His Golden Rules for business were so important to Penney that he named his first store in Kemmerer, Wyoming, *The Golden Rule*.

Here are Penney's five Golden Rules for operating a business:

1) Charge a fair price and receive a fair profit for what we offer.
2) Serve the public to its complete satisfaction.
3) Offer the best quality and value for the money.
4) Strive for a high level of intelligent and helpful service.
5) Make sure our actions square with what is right and just.

Basically, you can sum up Penney's business philosophy in one word: *Integrity*. My dictionary defines integrity as "the state of being of sound moral principle," which is a fancy way of saying that people with integrity make it a point to do the right thing at all times to all people, even when it's uncomfortable.

Compassionate Capitalism

J.C. Penney's integrity as a human and as a businessman serves as a guiding light for everyone who seeks to become successful in the fullest sense of the word. He was a man of integrity who foresaw that honesty was not only the best policy, but it was *essential for long-term success in business and in life*. "Golden rule principles are just as necessary for operating a business profitably," Penney said, "as are trucks, typewriters, or twine."

Penney's ageless advice is especially true when it comes to building your networking business, for your success is based solely on your ability to get your prospects and distributors to trust you.

Liars and cheats may profit for a little while in this business, but over time, dishonesty and immorality will kill a networking business quicker than you can say *SA-8!*

In his best-selling book *Compassionate Capitalism*, Rich DeVos observes that the old-style exploitative capitalism practiced by the "robber barons" at the turn of the 20th century has gradually given way to today's compassionate capitalism — which is based on principles of fairness and integrity.

"People helping people help themselves," is the way DeVos defines compassionate capitalism, and he argues convincingly that helping people help themselves is much more compassionate and freeing than the government paying people for NOT working!

Do You Create Trust?

Hank and I have been married for 40 years now, and I'd have to say that integrity is a big reason our marriage has lasted. Like all couples, we have our differences, but one thing we have in common is trust. Because Hank is a man of integrity, I know what he stands for — I can count on him. Everyone knows that Hank is fair and honest and dependable.

It's been my observation that trust is the glue that bonds together every long-lasting distributorship. When the trust stops, the people stop working and that means the income stops, too. Integrity isn't just some nice-sounding word tossed around at seminars that you can conveniently forget when you return home. Integrity is indispensable to your success. Never, ever lose sight of that!

Practice Principle-Centered Leadership

Steven Covey talks a lot about principle-centered leadership, observing that leadership without values is like a compass without a needle. What would happen if you were depending on someone using a needleless compass to lead you out of a forest? You wouldn't continue to follow someone who was leading you around and around in circles, would you? Of course not — you'd look for a different leader or strike out on your own.

As you are well aware, our business is a business of duplication, and perhaps, in our business more than any other, leaders lead by example. If distributors conduct their business in a dishonest or unethical manner, guess what they are teaching their people to do? That's right, they're teaching them to build a business on the shifting sand of unethical short-term gain, as opposed to building their business on a rock-solid, long-term foundation based on Godly principles.

That's why I say you MUST place integrity at the center of your moral compass. Following the path of integrity isn't always easy ... or popular, for that matter. But in the long run, it will be the right direction for you and for your people. J. Lawton Collins summed up the importance of principle-centered leadership with this observation:

> *No matter how brilliant a man may be, he will never engender confidence in his subordinates if he lacks simple honesty and moral courage.*

Truer words were never spoken!

What Kind of Empire Are You Building?

In a very real sense, as you build your business, you are building an empire. It can be an evil empire, destined for failure, like communist Russia. Or it can be an empire of integrity, destined for success, like the distributorships of so many Diamonds. The only way to ensure that your empire grows and flourishes is to build it on Godly principles.

Now, I'm not just talking about following the letter of the law here. When I talk about living a life of integrity, I'm talking about going beyond the secular to obey a higher law, namely, God's law.

The law of the land, for example, says that pornography is legal and acceptable. But you'll never convince me that pornography is acceptable in God's eyes. As a wise person once said, "First there is the law. It must be obeyed. But *the law is the minimum*. Good men and women go beyond the law and conduct themselves ethically at all times."

The law is the minimum — what a great line! Just because something is the law of the land doesn't make it right, isn't that true? I'm not suggesting you break laws. I'm suggesting that *the law is the minimum* and that you go beyond the law and do what is right. I'm suggesting you go beyond the minimum and build your business on integrity ... your relationships on integrity ... your marriage on integrity ... and your life on integrity.

Rev. John Wesley, founder of the Methodist Church, offers up a six-line prescription for living a life of integrity. With apologies to the late reverend, I have altered his words slightly to turn his words of wisdom into a personal "Pledge of Integrity." This is what I'm talking about when I say, "Integrity begins with an I:"

Personal Pledge of Integrity

I pledge to do all the good I can,
In all the ways I can,
In all the places I can,
At all times I can,
To all the people I can,
As long as ever I can.

Lesson 9:
A Lesson In Loyalty and Edification

> *It is better to be faithful than famous.*
> — Theodore Roosevelt

I'm very aware that, for many Americans, loyalty is a hopelessly old-fashioned notion. Today we celebrate individuality ... we admire independence ... we honor our differences ... we're encouraged to "run your own show" and "do your own thing."

Loyalty has been replaced by the clarion call of our age: *"What's in it for me?"*

Centuries ago, when Judas asked the Roman authorities the same question, "What's in it for me?" They answered, "30 pieces of silver." Judas took the money and ran, and as a result of his choosing money over loyalty, he became the most famous traitor in the history of the world. Whatever temporary satisfaction Judas received was short-lived, however. He committed suicide shortly after betraying Jesus.

A House Divided Cannot Stand

The story of Judas is a timeless lesson about the importance of loyalty: When we choose to put our own selfish, short-term interests above everyone else, disaster soon follows. The Bible warns us that "a house divided cannot stand," — a phrase often evoked by Abraham Lincoln to rally support for the union — and both the Old and the New Testaments are filled with stories and parables extolling the virtues of loyalty.

Loyalty is especially important in networking, for without loyalty, your organization can eventually disintegrate. Unlike network marketing, traditional businesses use "the power of the paycheck" to keep their employees in line and "loyal" to the company. We've all had jobs where we had to do things we thought were unproductive, or even downright silly, but we gritted our teeth and went along with the program so we could keep receiving that paycheck.

Networking, on the other hand, is a whole different deal. Your upline can't threaten to *fire you* because he or she didn't *hire you* in the first place! But if you are loyal to your upline ... to the corporation ... to the system ... and to the products — and if you teach your distributors to be loyal to you in turn — then you are laying the foundation for your business to grow and grow.

Build and Maintain Your Relationships

Relationships are everything in this business. You can't have a rock-solid relationship without trust, and you can't have trust without loyalty. Loyalty is the glue that holds every networking organization together.

Loyalty has a special meaning in my life because I saw what it did for me and my family, both during and after the war. When I was separated from my parents in Africa, for example, I knew in my heart that my parents would find me or they would die trying because our bond of loyalty was so strong that nothing short of death could break it. It took my mother months to track me down — and she had to overcome huge obstacles and thousands of miles in the process — but her relentless loyalty won out in the end.

How did I repay her loyalty? By rebelling against her parental authority! (I never said loyalty was always easy!) Thanks to my mother's patience and understanding, we weathered the brief storm in our relationship, and it wasn't long before I grew out of my rebellious phase.

My mother understood that loyalty doesn't come and go depending on your mood. Loyalty is a marathon, not a sprint. Loyalty means you carry an umbrella to protect you when it rains, and if you forget your umbrella, well, then it means you both get wet together. That's what loyalty is all about — remaining true through the ups and the downs, the bad times as well as the good.

Loyalty: The Essence of Teamwork

Loyalty isn't just a nice-sounding idea. It's not the management fad of the moment, either. Loyalty is a timeless concept based on Godly principles. When there is no loyalty, relationships disintegrate and chaos reigns. Without loyalty, families break up, former partners sue each other, employees cheat their employers, and countries engage in civil wars.

The Bible warns us against placing our self-interests ahead of others with these immortal words: "Pride comes before the fall." When people become so self-centered that they refuse to subjugate themselves to something larger than just themselves, then "the fall" is inevitable.

It follows that loyalty is the essence of teamwork, and teamwork is the backbone of our business. It's important for you to become independent in our business, but it's *essential that you become interdependent*. In other words, when you network, you aren't playing an individual sport like tennis, where your success depends entirely on your singular efforts. Rather, you're playing a team sport like football, where your success depends on everyone pulling together and making a positive contribution.

When you are building a team, there comes a time when you have to put the team's purpose and goals above your own. Sometimes you have to sacrifice what you think is best for YOU in order to do what is best for EVERYONE ON THE TEAM. And let's face it, it's no fun to put your ego in your back pocket, so to speak. But that's what teamwork is all about, isn't it? — putting the team's interest above your own self-interest. The only way to maximize your efforts in networking is to put the team first. The old saying "There's no 'I' in the word TEAM" is right on the money!

Make Your Spouse Part of Your Team

Hank and I are a living testimony to the power of teamwork. When we first started working the business, we were going nowhere fast. I thought the business should be done this way. He thought it should be done that way. We spent more time arguing over the way to build the business than we did actually building it!

Then one day, all of that changed. I was telling Hank that our dream of financial freedom was crumbling right in front of us, that maybe this business didn't work after all. Hank put a fire under our dream when he said, "Honey, this business works, and I know we can build it. From now on, you make one contact, and I'll make one contact. We'll build this business together."

From that moment forward, we have worked as a team. We were no longer two separate people pulling in two separate directions. We became a team pulling in the same direction. The business was no longer HIS business or MY business, it was OUR business. That adjustment in strategy, more than anything else, is the reason we were able to reach Diamond in five years, working part-time.

Oh, sure, we've had our disagreements from time to time. But we've learned to expect disagreements, even welcome them, in fact, because when we disagree, we usually come up with a solution that was better than either one of the original propositions! We're much better problem solvers today because we make decisions that are best for the team, as opposed to what is best for only one member of the team.

Now, I'm not saying you can't build a business without your spouse agreeing to be part of the team. I've seen a few people reach Diamond despite the fact their spouse fought them every step of the way. But believe me, it's a lot easier — and a lot more rewarding — when you have two people pulling the wagon in the same direction.

Edification: Building Up Your Upline

One of the best ways to practice what you preach about loyalty is to *edify* your upline at every opportunity. Edification means you build up your upline whenever you talk to others. Why? When you edify your upline, they can help you so much more because people will respect them and listen to what they have to say.

The word *edify* comes from the Latin word *aedes*, which meant a dwelling, a house, or a temple. (The English word *edifice*, which means a large, imposing building, comes from the same Latin root). When we edify others, then, we build them up, just as a contractor would build a house from the foundation up to the roof.

Edification is the application of the old expression, "If you can't say anything nice about someone, don't say anything at all." The purpose of edification is to present someone in their best light. That doesn't mean, of course, that you misrepresent people or lie about them. That's unethical and unnecessary.

When you edify someone, you're choosing to concentrate on the things a person does right, rather than what a person does wrong. And let's face it — you pretty much find what you look for in others. If you are determined to find fault with a person, guess what — the faults will spring out like flowers after a spring rain. Fortunately, just the opposite happens when we train ourselves to look for the positive traits in people.

The Value of Edification

Edification is one of the most powerful tools you have to build your business. Here's why: When you talk to your friends and family about the business, they're going to be a lot more skeptical of what you have to say than someone they've never met. To paraphrase the Bible, "A prophet is never recognized in his own town."

But when an "expert" speaks, the message gets through loud and clear. That's why the Diamonds travel around the country holding open meetings and major events. The Diamonds have earned their right to speak, and by building them up in the eyes of others, you are, in turn, building up yourself and the business.

When you edify your upline, you are, in effect, advertising your business in the same way that McDonald's or Ford advertises their businesses. When these companies advertise on TV, you won't hear the announcer criticize McDonald's hamburgers as being bad for your heart, will you? And you won't hear the Ford commercial criticizing their president for making lousy management decisions, will you? Of course not.

The purpose of advertising is to cast a product or company in a positive light. The same goes for our business. The difference is our business is advertised by word of mouth instead of in the media. Each time you say something to someone about the business or about your upline, you are advertising, so you always want to edify the people who will help you build your business, namely, your upline.

Edification is just one of the ways you express your loyalty in our business. As you build your business over time, you'll discover for yourself how the Biblical principles of loyalty and edification pay off. To paraphrase the great American author James Baldwin, "People have never been very good at listening to their superiors. But they have never failed to imitate them."

When you practice loyalty and edification, you are teaching your people to do the same, and they, in turn, will be teaching their new distributors to do the same, and so on and so on. In the long run, your loyalty to the team will return to you 10-fold. In the words of Mary Lou Retton, 1984 Olympic gold medal winner in gymnastics: "For me the word TEAM stands for Together Everyone Achieves More."

Lesson 10:
Leaving Your Legacy

We make a living by what we get.
But we make a life by what we give.
— Winston Churchill

I've known what I wanted my legacy to the world to be since I was seven years old — to deliver the message of freedom to all oppressed people in the world. I never wanted anyone to experience the misery I was being forced to endure, and I was determined to do my part to make the world a freer place to live.

As an adult I delivered my message to anyone who would listen. I was often asked to speak for clubs, schools, and civic groups, telling my story and encouraging Americans to cherish and protect their freedoms. I must say I became a bit of a local celebrity, and I did my share of talks on radio and TV.

But I was frustrated. I was telling my story to lots of people, but I didn't feel I was changing very many lives. I needed a vehicle that would enable me to spread my message and dramatically improve people's lives in the process.

Then, in 1972, Hank and I were introduced to the perfect vehicle for my message of freedom — the Amway business. The business gave me an opportunity to speak to audiences of hundreds . . . thousands . . . even tens of thousands of people at a time! Not only that, we were able to teach people a system whereby they could achieve their freedom, and they, in turn, could teach others the same system, and so on and so on. In a sense, Hank and I became disciples, spreading our message of freedom to anyone and everyone who would listen.

Family Comes First

When Hank and I first looked at the business, I was in my late 30s and Hank was in his early 40s, and we saw it mainly as a means to an end — a way to help us reach our goal of financial freedom by helping others do the same. But the longer we worked the business, the more we grew to appreciate some other benefits, such as personal growth and the joy of being surrounded by positive people. One of the biggest side benefits of the business is the fact that it's inheritable.

Hank and I didn't initially build the business with the idea of passing it along to our children, but the older we got, the more we came to appreciate the inheritable aspect of the business. Our son Mark works with us full-time now, and we are priming him for the day when he takes the reins of our distributorship, just as the children of Rich DeVos and Jay Van Andel have made the successful transition to running the day-to-day operations of Amway Corporate.

Hank and I believe that the biggest part of our legacy is to our family, for they are our first line of responsibility. We did our best to leave our children with a legacy of positive values and Godly principles that they, in turn, would pass on to their children. Have you heard the old saying, "When you teach your children, you are teaching your children's children's children"? It's true. Values can be passed on through the generations just as surely as physical traits.

Our priorities in life are God, family, and country, in that order, and if everyone in the world had the same priorities, 99 percent of the social workers — including police officers, prison guards, and welfare case workers — would be out of a job tomorrow. The first legacy that everyone should seek to leave to their children is the legacy of decency and independence.

Our Children Grow Up in the Business

Our two sons have been exposed to so much more than the average person because of our involvement in the business. They've learned key success principles by reading books and listening to speeches on free enterprise and personal growth, and they've associated with hundreds of positive, successful people. As a result of the principles and values that Michael and Mark learned in the business, both of them are in business for themselves.

Our older son, Michael, and his wife, Peggy, are Amway distributors and own a successful construction company, MPG Builders. We've watched Michael grow and mature over the years, and we are so proud of him!

Our younger son, Mark, works with us full time and runs most of our business and ministry activities. The business has afforded Mark the opportunity to travel to more than 15 different countries around the world, from Mexico and Canada to mainland China and Hong Kong to Poland, Germany, and Portugal.

He runs our Youth Leadership Camps each summer here and in Europe, where we're helping to raise up the next generation of Godly leaders. The motto of our leadership camp is "We cannot always build the future for our youth, but we can build our youth for the future."

Mark has turned into quite a leader himself. He's given countless seminars all over the world, from Poland to China. He's had the opportunity to meet his heroes in person, people like Arnold Schwarzeneggar, Ronald Reagan, George Bush, Billy Graham, and many others. Mark and his friend Billy Childers (son of a supersuccessful Executive Diamond in the business) even had the opportunity to work at the White House during George Bush's administration, and Mark has become close friends with many other second-generation leaders in the business.

Mark is concentrating on touching lives all over the world through the business and through various ministries, and we feel certain our legacy will live on through our children.

What Happens When You Leave?

Peter Drucker is a world-famous management expert who has consulted for most of the Fortune 500 companies and written scores of best-selling books. In a recent interview in *INC* Magazine, Drucker was asked this question: "Businesspeople are good at turning short-term profits, but what are we doing [in business] that's good enough to last?"

"The only thing that matters is how you touch people," Drucker answered thoughtfully. "The test of a leader is not what happens during his lifetime, but what happens when he leaves."

I think Drucker hit the nail right on the head with his answer because it strikes at the heart of what a legacy is and why it is so important: *The test of a leader is not what happens in his lifetime, but what happens when he leaves.*

That statement pretty much sums up not just the legacy of a successful businessperson, but the legacy of every single person who ever walked the earth. Our test is not what happens in this lifetime, but what we leave the world when we are gone.

Time to Give Back

Hank and I are at the stage in our lives when we can afford to give back to people who didn't have the opportunities that we have had in this country. Giving back is the main reason we are continuing to help people build their businesses.

Once Hank and I achieved financial independence, our definition of success started to change. We still respect the power of money, of course, and we're still motivated to continue building a solid, profitable business. But for us, success is less and less about making money and more and more about leaving a legacy.

In the words of Hector Cantu, author of *Do You Have Time for Success?*, "Success has less to do with money than with reaching your maximum potential and helping people along the way." The beauty of our business is you can do all three of those things at the same time — you can make money, maximize your potential, and help people! WOW! That's a win, win, win situation!

Trickle Down Theory

Do you remember when President Reagan coined the phrase, the "trickle down theory." In short, the theory says that when you cut the taxes of the top income earners, their tax savings trickle down to everybody in the economy because they'll have more money to spend and invest. When a rich person buys a new Mercedes, for example, the money trickles down from buyer to the salesman who earns a bigger commission ... to the contractor who builds the salesman's new home ... to the roofers, plumbers, and carpenters who earn more money by working more hours ... to the stores that sell food and clothes to the carpenter's kids ... and so on. In short, a rising tide raises all boats.

Money isn't the only thing that trickles down and gets passed around. Attitudes trickle down, too. So do behaviors. And values. And dreams.

I remember sharing the stage with Dr. Norman Vincent Peale years ago, and I had an opportunity to talk with him backstage. I was awestruck by his youthful enthusiasm and his passion for his calling. I could feel my spirit and attitude soar as I talked to Dr. Peale. I glowed for days afterward, and I passed that glow on to everyone I came in contact with. I'm sure that many of those people who caught my positive enthusiasm passed it along to people they came in contact with, and thus, it trickled down, influencing people I would never, ever meet in person.

The point is that you don't have to die to leave a legacy to someone. And that legacy doesn't have to be money in the form of an inheritance or a trust fund. Every single one of us leaves a living legacy every day of our lives. That legacy can be a concept — like freedom. Or an emotion — like love. Or a lesson — like "Before you can receive, first you must give." Or a book you recommend to a friend — like *The Magic of Thinking Big*. These may seem like small, insignificant gestures, but you never know when an unexpected kindness or a timely suggestion can dramatically change someone's life, who, in turn, will pass your wisdom on to others, and so on down the line.

Go Light Your World

One of my favorite songs begins and ends with this lyric:

> *There is a candle in every soul ...*
> *Take your candle and go light your world.*

I believe with all my heart that everyone has a candle that can help light the way for others who follow. It's up to each of us to light our candle and pass it along.

With my candle I seek to light the path that leads people to freedom — total, glorious freedom. It's my special living legacy to the world, and I'll carry the candle of freedom wherever I go, and I pray its light will burn bright and steady long, long after I have left this world.

But what about you? Have you thought about the candle in your soul? Do you know what it is? Have you thought about what you will leave the world when you are no longer here? Will your legacy endure? Will it be positive? Will it be something that will make you proud? Will it make the world a better place?

My friend, my life is proof that one person can make a difference. So can you. You can touch a soul in pain ... say a kind word ... reach down and help someone in need ... pass on a value ... leave a legacy you can be proud of.

Look inside yourself.

Discover your special candle.

And then take your candle and light your world.

Conclusion:
A Truimphant Return

Warsaw, Poland, November 1992

"**L**adies and gentlemen," our host announced, "let's give a great big Polish welcome to Hank and Alicia Gilewicz!"

The audience jumped to their feet and cheered. I squeezed Hank's hand and blinked back tears as we walked onto the stage of the packed auditorium in Warsaw, Poland.

We had traveled thousands of miles from our comfortable home in South Carolina to deliver a message to the Polish people. My hand trembled as I gripped the microphone, but my voice was strong and steady:

"Dreams really can come true," I said. *"You and I — everyone in this room — are living proof that DREAMS REALLY CAN COME TRUE!"*

The audience stood and cheered. All I could do was smile and wave — and cry.

I cried for the Polish people who were forced to endure 50 years of brutal oppression under the communists.

I cried for the six million Polish citizens who were murdered in WWII.

I cried for my lost childhood, for the pain and the sadness are still with me today.

But most of all, I cried tears of joy — I had finally returned to a free Poland. It took 50 years and cost millions of lives, but finally, finally, Poland was free!

My life had come full circle since that cold, gray morning when the soldiers marched my parents and me out of our home. The frozen footprints we left in the snow melted away years and years ago. Now it was my turn to help the Polish people melt their frozen footprints by lighting the fire of free enterprise within their hearts.

My life is proof that faith and free enterprise will triumph in the end. My life is proof that dreams really can come true.

This book is my story of freedom. I challenge you to create your own story of freedom.

Start by melting the frozen footprints in your life.

That's when you'll begin to discover that dreams — *your dreams* — really can come true!